THE SIX PILLARS APPROACH WORKS

Thanks to Mr. Dade for simplifying an overwhelming digital landscape with clear, concise advice and a touch of dry wit.

DARIN LEE , DIRECTOR OF SHOPPER MARKETING

This crash course goes beyond helping marketers...even those on the vendor or technology side gain valuable insights into the in-depth decision making process and buying requirements that create standout winners in the space.

BLAKE DECOLA, SENIOR DIRECTOR OF CPG AND
SHOPPER MARKETING

I've been involved in shopper marketing sales for over ten years and never have I found such an all-encompassing guide to help break down the numerous strategies that go into campaign execution. [This] should be required reading for anyone navigating the shopper marketing world.

MEREDITH WILLIAMS, DIRECTOR OF DIGITAL
BUSINESS DEVELOPMENT & PATH-TO-PURCHASE
INSTITUTE WOMEN OF EXCELLENCE HONOREE

THE SIX PILLARS APPROACH WORKS

A fantastic read for any current or future shopper marketer. A very thoughtful approach that dives deeper into a shopper marketer's decision-making."

ZACHARY PLUNKETT, SENIOR CLIENT DIRECTOR

A must read for marketers and sellers alike.

HUNTER POOLE, ACCOUNT EXECUTIVE

Use [the Six Pillars] Approach and become a shopper marketing rock star!

CHRIS W. TEN NAPEL, PARTNER - DIGITAL SALES

This book provides a blueprint for driving shopper marketing in a digital age at any budget.

ASHLEY MURDTER, SENIOR ACCOUNT DIRECTOR

SHOPPER MARKETING AND DIGITAL MEDIA

SIMPLIFYING YOUR DIGITAL MEDIA PLANS WITH THE SIX PILLARS APPROACH

F.M. DADE

STAR WHEEL
B O O K S

Shopper Marketing and Digital Media: Simplifying Your Digital Media Plans With The Six Pillars Approach by F.M. Dade. Published by Star Wheel Books. © 2020.

© 2020 Star Wheel Books. www.StarWheelBooks.com

For information about special discounts available for bulk purchases or media coverage, contact publisher@starwheelbooks.com.

Cover illustration by Star Wheel Books. Book formatting by Vellum. Used by permission. All rights reserved.

ISBN 978-1-7333472-7-3 (ebook)

ISBN 978-1-7333472-8-0 (paperback)

ISBN 978-1-7333472-9-7 (hardcover)

First edition.

For all of the companies, brands, and teams that trusted me to push their business forward.

CONTENTS

PRICING

PAST PERFORMANCE

DIGITAL MEDIA TOOLS IN A SHOPPER MARKETING WORLD

THE SIX PILLARS APPROACH EXERCISES

To be successful in digital, you must be comfortable being uncomfortable.

MY FIRST BOSS IN DIGITAL MEDIA

INTRODUCTION

Very few things in the world of marketing have as many accepted definitions as shopper marketing. Chris Hoyt, long-time CPG marketer and founder of Hoyt & Co., famously describes it as "brand marketing in [a] retailer environment." Early shopper marketing powerhouse Unilever highlights the importance of "shopper insights" as a foundational element in shopper marketing. Unilever defines a "shopper insight" as "the process that takes place between that first thought the consumer has about purchasing the item, all the way through the selection of the item." The discipline of shopper marketing challenges the long-held belief that the consumer and the shopper are the same. For instance, think about the person in your own household who consumes the potato chips. Is that the same person who is actually buying them? Maybe. Maybe not. Shopper marketing wants to address and influence the *shopper*—the one in the store, on the site, or in the app—making the actual purchase. And that approach is going to look different for every retail account. At the end of the day, driving conversions at a specific retailer for your brand, using insights that you have on that shopper, are the essence of shopper marketing.

The origins of shopper marketing are traced back to the early 2000s when, depending on the story you believe, either Coca-Cola or Procter & Gamble first openly used the term. As to the claim of who was responsible for the term itself, it may have been Sam's Club executive Rhonda Harper at a joint planning session with hundreds of Procter & Gamble marketers and sales executives, or it could have been the more widely accepted answer of Chris Hoyt in 2006. But it wasn't until 2010 that a formal definition of shopper marketing was outlined by the Retail Commission on Shopper Marketing:

> Shopper Marketing is the use of insights-driven marketing and merchandising initiatives to satisfy the needs of targeted shoppers, enhance the shopping experience and improve business results and brand equity for retailers and manufacturers.

As shopper marketing proved itself to be an area of growth, more and more dollars were funneled toward this account-specific work. Though every company approached it a bit differently, the common theme was that you absolutely needed to do it. This rather quick adoption led to multiple interpretations and various levels of success. But, twenty years later, shopper marketing is still very much a staple of nearly every consumer packaged goods (CPG) company and is continuing to evolve.

Two of the biggest misconceptions about shopper marketing throughout the years have been 1) the notion that it is exclusively in-store advertising such as shelf flags, floor decals, coupon machines, end card headers, and the like, and 2) that all shopper marketing has to be promotion focused and include a coupon or a rebate or a special deal.

The first one is definitely not true. If it were, you wouldn't be reading this book. Digital media and advertising have been impacting shoppers in the lower part of the funnel for some time now, driving them in-store to purchase, as well as online.

The second one is also false. You don't need a promotion to have an insights-driven campaign targeting a retailer's shopper with the goal of driving an immediate short-term return at that retailer. Can a coupon or a retailer-specific promotion help? Yes, sometimes. It can also hurt your performance. Remember, the word *marketing* is in the term *shopper marketing*, and not everything is simply a matter of trade or pricing.

For the majority of its early days, however, shopper marketing *was* primarily an in-store activity due to the fact that digital hadn't really become a major avenue to market CPGs. Also, Procter & Gamble's first moment of truth (FMOT) narrative, developed in 2005, caught on like wildfire. FMOT can be defined as when consumers are standing in front of the actual product. And when P&G backs something, the rest of the CPG world follows. In-store advertising and marketing from vendors such as News America Marketing, Insignia POPS, and Valassis became the hottest new marketing toy. Years later, a zero moment of truth was amended to the philosophy: when consumers/shoppers are doing their research. And shopper marketing quickly entered the digital media realm.

The nascent phase of digital shopper marketing centered around promotions such as digital coupons. Coupons, Inc. (now Quotient Technology) and News America Marketing duked it out over retailers' print-at-home coupon business, with Coupons, Inc. winning out and building "walled gardens" around the retailer sites. In 2006, Giant Eagle pioneered the first download-to-card or direct-to-card (D2C) coupons, whereby consumers could load their offers onto their loyalty card. Once again, Coupons, Inc. won out, dominating that side of the digital promotions equation as well.

But in the early 2010s, the alluring presence of digital display media (also known as banner ads) caught the eye of shopper marketers all over the industry. MaxPoint Interactive, one of the early winners in the shopper marketing-centric digital media space, helped push shopper marketers into considering "real" digital media (no promotions) to support their brands at a given retailer. Then, in 2013,

MaxPoint partnered with Retail Solutions, Inc. to create what would become the industry's first shopper marketing digital display campaign optimized on real-time point-of-sale (POS) sales data, with an incremental sales measurement with statistical significance to boot. This was a paradigm shifting moment as shopper marketers were scrambling to learn an entirely new industry: adtech (advertising technology). Needless to say, it hasn't been a flawless marriage as in-store marketing and digital media are strange bedfellows to say the least. Because of this, classically trained shopper marketers—that is to say, those who felt more comfortable in the world of "shelftalkers" and neck hangers, farmed out their digital buys to shopper marketing agencies (because agencies should know digital, right?), or even worse, just went with what was easiest. Some even just slapped a retailer logo on national buys, geo-targeted the ads around stores, and called it shopper marketing. No shopper insights. No anything. The industry was left with years and years of poorly executed programs that couldn't definitively say if the campaign had succeeded or failed.

It was and *still is* unrealistic to ask shopper marketers to be experts on two distinct industries—in-store marketing/promotions and ad tech/digital media—they are both complex and evolving. What this book aims to do is simply take the scary world of digital media and its vast nuances and reduce them to digestible chunks, removing the shiny objects that lead us down a path of distraction. A simple methodology, such as the Six Pillars Approach, can give a shopper marketer the tools for planning a high-performing, conceptually sound digital media program without having to spend a decade learning the adtech ecosystem and its many offshoots.

I hope this way of thinking can help you as it has helped me, as well as other marketers in the industry.

THE SIX PILLARS
APPROACH

THREE CHALLENGES OF THE MODERN SHOPPER MARKETER

As a modern shopper marketer, you are either tasked with being an expert in digital media or being a trusted evaluator of how the money is being allocated and measured by your agency of choice. It's not a fair ask, assuming that you aren't sacrificing your other day-to-day jobs such as in-store marketing, managing promotions, building a relationship with the buyer, communicating plans cross-functionally across your organization—and the entire list of internal duties and projects. More often than not, you are doing the work of two or three people as a shopper marketing lead and the digital media portion is likely the largest cause of your angst and constant head spinning.

In a perfect world, to be an expert, you must have a working mastery of the following three topics.

Know the Digital Media and Ad Tech Space

Yes, the big one. Not only understanding the history of online advertising—from exclusively publisher-direct models to ad networks to the rise of programmatic buying—but all of the topics that make up the most convoluted nook residing in marketing: deterministic versus probabilistic; viewability; machine-based learning; real-time bidding; cross-device graphs; ad fraud and non-human traffic; domain-level safety versus page-level safety; in-stream versus outstream versus in-banner; paid social versus organic social; multitouch attribution; conversion pathways and sequencing; dynamic creative optimization —you get the picture, right?

Don't beat yourself up over only knowing the answers to a few of these. You're not supposed to, at least not right out of the gate. Some of these will be addressed in this book in a very simple and manageable manner. Others simply don't have a major effect on your programming (regardless of what the vendors say). It has taken many of us years and years of being fully committed to the digital landscape to become experts or to have more than a working knowledge. It's no different from your mastery of the non-digital media components of shopper marketing. Do you think digital marketers could come in right away and plan retailtainment events or demos or shelf signs in the most optimal way? Or, even more, try and leverage spend to get incremental merchandising in the store? They wouldn't know the first thing about installation compliance and shelf resets and redemption liability. But the reality is that very few digital marketers are having their roles augmented with these responsibilities; and you, as a shopper marketer, *are* having the scope of your job descriptions widened to include digital.

Understand Digital Media in Shopper Marketing

Unfortunately, it's not as simple as just knowing digital media. You have to be comfortable in a niche of a niche: CPG shopper-marketing-specific digital media. Since it's so specific, you can focus on just a few simple areas, right? Yes and no. Yes, this book will help guide you to the biggest and most critical questions to effectively plan your digital media. No, it's not entirely devoid of overarching digital media principles. You will need to know what deterministic and probabilistic data is to be able to make the call on which one to pursue for a certain campaign. But you don't need to understand every step in the direct matching process that a vendor undertakes necessarily. Many of the fancier or sexier components of the broader adtech landscape simply won't apply to shopper marketing, not due to the size of budgets or relative importance to an organization, but because primary success metrics are pretty black and white and the relationships with retailers and their data limit some of the attribution models that are so present in verticals such as retail or nonprofit or auto.

When you are done with the Six Pillar Approach, not only will you be able to plan your digital media buys more effectively but you will actually know some digital things that your friends in national media or on the programmatic buying team won't—and make sure to rub it in every time you see them at the next company happy hour!

Keep Up with Changes in the E-Commerce Landscape

Of the three, this is the task that is probably already part of your gig to some degree. By the very nature of shopper marketing, you are concerned with the shoppers at your retailer, whether they are more prone to purchase in-store or more apt to order online. By the time the publisher hits print on this book, I'm sure even more changes will have occurred in this space. However, there are some truths that I do believe will remain relevant over the foreseeable future. First, click-and-collect/curbside pickup as well as home delivery will continue to grow. It might not be as fast as during the early stages of the 2020 COVID-19 pandemic, but it will continue to tick upward until we reach a tipping point and migrate to dark stores. Not sure if that will happen in the next decade, but you never know. Secondly, more (and smaller) retailers will add on conversion channels such as pick up, home delivery, and national ship. This is fairly obvious, but the bigger question is if they will develop these infrastructures natively or rely on third parties such as Instacart or Drizly. This choice impacts your ability to market to that retailer's shopper versus the third-party platform's shopper. Lastly, as retailer's see volume shift to their sites and apps, they will continue to push you for more dollars with their retailer media network offerings. There is an entire chapter on the evils and opportunities within the retailer media network space but, needless to say, the role of retailer media offering expert will likely fall on you. Beyond the movement in e-commerce from a retailer standpoint, there will also be new technologies that are specific to your role, such as auto-add-to-cart. More on that later.

These three challenges look pretty scary—and they should. It's a lot. It's a lot even if you didn't do all of that other stuff you do. Ya' know, traditional shopper marketing. However, the reality is you must embrace it and become skilled at thoughtfully planning your digital programming. If you can do this, the value that you will bring to your organization *and the retailer* will be immense. The Six Pillars Approach is that first step.

The Myth of Always-Changing Media as a Roadblock

Before we get into the approach itself, I want to address the elephant in the room: the prevailing notion that digital media is changing with every blink of an eye. Why should you spend any time reading a book that will be considered a dinosaur by the time you finish it. I know you're thinking it.

This book is *not* a capabilities overview of all of the top digital tactics and vendors in the space, though we do discuss the merits of certain digital tactics throughout. This is not meant to be a guide about the latest breakthrough in cross-device matching or ad fraud identification. Your vendor partners will be more than happy to share those advancements in product over a nice, free lunch. These changes and upgrades to capabilities are *absolutely always changing*. Every day, a vendor partner tweaks this or removes that to make a slightly better mousetrap. No one on the planet can be up to speed on every tiny improvement in the world of adtech. You don't need that to be a stellar digital shopper marketer.

What this book does is lay out an approach to plan your digital media buys in a streamlined and focused manner, de- cluttering the messy world of digital media to make sense for your specific campaign. This approach made sense in 2010 and it will make sense in 2050 because it cuts through the noise to build a campaign that answers your primary objective, whatever that may be. In that regard, it is evergreen in nature.

With this unwavering and timeless framework, the inclusion of foundational elements of digital media will be pulsed into the decisioning process. These pillars, as they will be referred to here, are also evergreen. They are the same pillars that I used when working with dozens of CPGs in 2013 on their digital shopper marketing programming and they haven't changed here in 2020. What *did* change was the material that made up the pillar: the updates and upgrades made across the industry that addressed that particular pillar. For example, the data pillar has always been important and will continue to be, but the data that we have access to and that could potentially identify a Walmart shopper has evolved drastically over time. You don't need to be an expert on every aspect of the material in order to use the pillar effectively; you just need to know when and how to stand that pillar up to support your objective.

THE ROOF AND PILLARS SYSTEM

For many shopper marketers (and digital marketers as well), the most daunting task of their job is to try and compare and evaluate the dozens and dozens of potential vendor partners and tactics that flood the digital media landscape. You are constantly inundated with cleverly phrased and expertly delivered pitches on secret sauces and "why we are different from our competitors." It's enough to make your head spin. It shouldn't be. First and foremost, you are probably being bombarded with nuanced differences that have very little, if any, material impact on your business. That's not to say that some vendor partners aren't better than others. Some are unequivocally better, but the real question should be which of these vendor partners gives me the best opportunity to achieve my campaign objective? Once you identify that, it gets easier. I promise. But even the answer to that question can only be achieved if you have a solid *yet flexible* foundation—that is, if you have a way to evaluate a vendor that can be used across KPIs and tactics.

I spent many years trying, on both the vendor and client side of the house, to isolate what really matters when it comes to selecting the right digital partner for a shopper marketing campaign. I wanted to simplify the process and eliminate the ability for caveats and special factors, but I didn't want one aspect to trump another. Data isn't more important than media unless that particular campaign won't achieve its objective without it. Technology isn't more important than pricing unless that particular campaign cannot succeed without it. Get the picture?

I have been using this approach in my day jobs for a few years and it has been successful beyond my wildest dreams. Not only is it easily digestible, even to a digital media novice, but it has helped a lot of already smart people make even smarter decisions—and feel confident in those decisions.

I introduce to you the **Six Pillars Approach**.

These six simple and broad (by design) criteria points—**data**, **technology**, **media**, **attribution**, **pricing**, and **past performance**—help marketers cut through the digital fluff and salesperson sizzle to get to what matters. It can be used to help you select the right digital tactic *and* the right vendor, all in one process.

Establishing the Roof

Before you start putting up the pillars, you need to establish the roof that the pillars support. The roof is made up of two critical elements: 1) your key performance indicator (KPI) or campaign objective, and 2) the message that you are conveying to achieve that objective.

The top of the roof, the most important part, is the KPI. What are you trying to accomplish and what will make this campaign be deemed a success or a failure? Are you being tasked with generating incremental sales at your retailer in an efficient manner and producing a strong gross margin return on investment (GMROI)? Is it to get as many add-to-carts on a retailer's click-and-collect platform during key seasonality? Is it to increase household penetration on your brand at the retailer?

Before you can plan any marketing effort, digital or otherwise, you need to have a clear KPI. And only one. KPI alignment stands at the vanguard of the Six Pillars Approach. Every decision should ladder up directly to this objective. The well-placed question Does this help me achieve my KPI of [insert your KPI here]? will be a valuable ally in your planning process.

The base of the roof, just below the KPI layer, is the message itself. That is to say, what is the message that I am trying to convey in order to achieve my KPI? Sometimes this is dictated by the national campaign or a new innovation or product attribute; sometimes this is 100% customized to the retailer. Either way, it is necessary to account for the message type in order to select a tactic.

If you are telling shoppers about a new flavor, you could possibly do this effectively with a static digital display ad. The creative limitations of the tactic won't be a roadblock to communicating the flavor extension to a shopper. If you are trying to communicate an alternative usage occasion for your product, then your static banner ad probably won't cut it. You might need to pursue longer-form media such as video or influencers.

When you are finished with the roof elements, you should be able to confidently say, "I am trying to achieve X by saying Y. I am trying to generate incremental sales by highlighting the organic benefits of my product. I am trying to increase frequency by showcasing my product as part of a recipe. I am trying to induce trial of my product by communicating a retailer promotion." All of these examples are solid roofs. Now we need something to prop the roof up!

Ranking the Pillars

The six pillars, themselves, can and should be weighted and prioritized, based on each individual campaign. This is where common-sense marketing comes into play. If your campaign goal is to increase frequency for your brand and drive the best GMROI, using examples of alternative usage occasions, it's imperative to target known existing brand buyers with a tactic that has the ability to communicate complex messages effectively. In that case, you might weight **data** higher so that you can make sure you aren't wasting impressions and money on non-brand buyers. You might have to pay more or sacrifice preferred optimization strategies or execute a tactic (or run with a vendor) that hasn't performed in the past. But if you are confident about the objective of increasing frequency, then the focus should squarely be on data so you can make sure you are serving ads to an existing brand buyer. Assuming that you have a few options that rise to the top of the data pillar, you can then go down the list, based on what you consider the next campaign priority. Eventually, you get to the right tactic and the right vendor.

Continuing with this example, let's say you have two tactics and five potential partners that meet your data needs to target those existing brand buyers. If we revisit the campaign objective of increasing frequency and producing a great GMROI, we notice that incremental generation, in the most efficient manner, is critical. We can address this in a few ways. First, let's look at **past perfor-mance** to see if there are any internal learnings from previous campaigns that might catapult a tactic to the top of the list of GMROI performers. For the sake of this exercise, past campaign metrics are not available. At this point, we dive deeper into common-sense marketing. Ask yourself, "Even though I know GMROI is important, do I need to share this metric with my management?" If so, we can focus on tactics that can provide us the necessary **attri-bution** so we can report on incremental sales, ideally with statistical significance.

Of those two tactics that met the data needs, only one possesses a partnership with an attribution vendor that can measure incremental sales on a campaign, which allows us to back into a GMROI. You have your tactic of choice! Now what? You have to ask yourself which of the two partners that can execute this recommended tactic will give you a better chance to hit and, hopefully exceed, that GMROI benchmark. Is it better to focus on **pricing** so you have more impres-sions out in the marketplace? Remember that the quality of the audience being served has already been addressed by the data pillar. Is it better to find a partner with the best **technology** to, in theory, drive better performance? Or what about the **media:** will the ads living on contextually relevant sites give you the best chance of generating incremental sales from your existing buyers? There isn't a wrong answer. It's part personal preference, part opportunity to test. But the best part is, at this point, that you have a tactic designated and are selecting a vendor partner that can confidently hit existing brand buyers and can accurately measure incremental sales (which allows you to back into a GMROI). You are 99.9% there and your next selection—be it pricing, technology, or media—should be viewed as an opportunity to test and learn.

To recap:
1. **Establish the roof.**
2. **Identify your campaign objective/KPI**: increase frequency of your brand; generate a strong GMROI.
3. **What message is going to help you achieve the objective?** Communication of alternative usage occasions; longer-form media to highlight effectively. After this stage, you should be able to eliminate tactics that can't communicate this message.
4. **Rank** the Six Pillars.
5. **Data,** because targeting known existing brand buyers is critical so impressions aren't wasted on nonbrand buyers.
6. **Past Performance:** you don't have any past campaigns to review.
7. **Attribution:** because you want to present statistically significant GMROI to your management team. After this stage, you likely have found your best tactic.
8. **Pricing** *or* **Technology** *or* **Media:** at this point, you can't really go wrong. You've set yourself up to find a vendor that can target the right audience (as described by your objective) and measure it. What do *you* think will help drive performance more: 1) lower

pricing/more impressions, an impressive AI-based platform that looks at 100,000 points of data (within your audience) to determine the shopper most likely to perform an action, or 2) premium sites where shoppers are going to plan their next trip? Ideally, you can test all of these over time, or if you have a strong performer, go back to the well, time and time again.

Visually, it should look something like this:

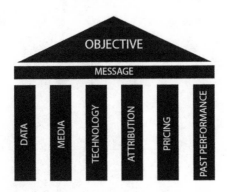

In addition, the matrix doesn't support or shun philosophical debates such as open audience targeting versus static segment targeting. As you will see, depending on the campaign objective, these targeting methodologies might align better or worse with a particular program. Adtech professionals love to argue theory, especially when it comes at the intersection of the marketing discipline and technological capabilities, and this matrix allows for those arguments to persist without muddying up the decision-making process.

Let's dive a bit deeper into each of the six pillars.

DATA

DATA

When you ask eager digital media sales reps about what separates them from the other 15,000 competitors (many of whom have sent you a cold email as you read this sentence), chances are that they reply with some variation of "It's our data." I'm not going to use this forum to review the validity of data sources, the death of the cookie, first party versus second party versus third party, deterministic versus probabilistic, and so on. because you should utilize a common-sense approach to data.

- Does it make sense?
- Does it originate from something you know about or makes sense to you?

For example, if a vendor tells me that the data comes from Kroger loyalty card data, I get that. I know which data is collected. I get why that data is relevant, and, heck, I probably own one of those cards. If another vendor tells me that it comes from a proprietary network of premium publishers that builds best-in-class purchase intent signals —and that's all they give me—then I immediately devalue that data.

Now, to be clear, in the Six Pillar system, data that is determined to be weak doesn't automatically remove it from the consideration set. It's one of six pillars, yes, but it might not be a crucial element to achieve the objective. Now, if the goal of the campaign is to grow households by targeting competitive brand buyers, then it could (and should) absolutely eliminate the proprietary network's data from the consideration set. Would you feel comfortable that the vendor who gave me that nebulous response is representing a tactic that could confidently hit competitive brand buyers? Nope.

Key Consideration Points

So what are major points to consider around data (and this is a very small snapshot of what could be important to you)?

- What are the data sources?
- How transparent is the partner with the sources?
- Are the sources syndicated, off-the-shelf, third-party segments?
- Are they custom segments?
- Is the data truly proprietary or exclusive? Is it purchase-based data? Demographic? Psychographic? Contextual/site visitation- based?
- What is the data chain of custody guard rails?
- Most importantly, if my objective requires me to talk to a certain type of shopper, does that data help me talk to that shopper?

Many times, in shopper marketing, data will be a primary pillar. Even if you are only targeting shoppers at a given retailer—with no brand or category overlay—you still have to make sure you aren't wasting impressions on a shopper who would, or has, never considered your supported retailer. However, to unequivocally assume data is the most important of all programs is just as faulty an assumption.

DETERMINISTIC VS. PROBABILISTIC

Your first day in digital media class—if something like a digital media class existed—would probably cover covering deterministic data versus probabilistic data. It's a foundational element of understanding data and targeting in a digital media world, including your *shopper marketing-centric* digital media world.

Having worked at one of the originators of people- based marketing—that is, using deterministic data to build actual profiles of people, without modeling or guesswork—I have a natural inclination to view this approach as the *only* approach. However, that statement is too sweeping and doesn't factor in key points such as pricing, availability/accessibility, and relevance to the campaign KPI.

Let's start with the basics.

Basics of Deterministic and Probabilistic Data

Deterministic data is a direct, confirmed match (1:1 match) of data, based on unique identifiers that were entered by the users themselves, such as an email address or a phone number. This data can be collected from websites, app log-ins, social media, newsletter sign-ups, online surveys, and so on. Since online users inputted the addressable identifier themselves, commonly referred to as declared data, it is considered 100% accurate—or deterministic.

Digital media companies can then take this known profile and match cookies and mobile IDs to it so additional information can be appended to this unique user. Of course, the personally identifiable information (PII) is encrypted using tools with hashing technology to meet legal regulations.

Another major advantage of deterministic data is the validation of a company's cross-device graph. As shoppers everywhere increase the number of devices that they use, brands have more opportunities to influence potential converters on laptops, mobile devices, tablets, gaming consoles, smart TVs, and so on. However, making sure you understand if you are sending an ad to the same person, but using a different device, is extremely important in reporting accurate reach and frequency. In addition, if your campaign is employing dynamic creative optimization or creative sequencing, this will be a necessity to achieve optimal performance.

Conversely, probabilistic data isn't 100% confirmed as true but has a high probability (as the name indicates) of accuracy. Probabilistic data and modeling are a hallmark of data scientists everywhere, where they build look-a-like segments using a large pool of data. So how does this work in the digital media world? Vendor partners can take anonymous data such as website visitation or device IDs to build out an audience profile. They can then apply that against the larger pool of cookies to determine what profiles closely resemble the original set.

PROBABILISTIC DATA

GENDER: Likely Female

GEOGRAPHY: Valdosta, GA

AGE: 18-35

MARITAL STATUS: Likely Married

DEVICES: ?

ONLINE BEHAVIOR:
· In-Market Travel
· In Market Auto
· Visited advertiser site

DETERMINISTIC DATA

GENDER: Female

GEOGRAPHY: Valdosta, GA 31601

AGE: 33

MARITAL STATUS: Married

CHILDREN: Yes, 2

DEVICES: Samsung Galaxy S20,
Playstation 4, Samsung 42" TV, MacBook Air

ONLINE BEHAVIOR:
· Frequent purchases at Kroger
· Shops at Buy, Buy, Baby
· Heavy purchaser of pasta sauce
· Watches Top Chef (Bravo)
· Subscribes to Food & Wine
· Membership at Lifetime Fitness
· Has been to the Atlanta Zoo 3x in last year

Deterministic data is always going to be more accurate because it's personally addressable and removes the need for look-a-like modeling. Even though deterministic is more accurate, it lacks the scale of probabilistic in many cases— and it you don't have scale, your accuracy might not be as important. Though it's improving versus a few years ago when there were only two or three deterministic data sets large enough to make an impact, the ability to tap into 100% deterministic data is not overly accessible. Companies such as Conversant Media and Viant have really challenged the "walled gardens" of Facebook, Google, and Amazon to the joy of marketers across the world.

For shopper marketers, the likelihood of needing to identify a retailer's shopper with near 100% certainty is crucial. Therefore, deterministic targeting is going to be your first choice—but you should never rule out probabilistic entirely. As mentioned earlier, factors such as the availability of the data that you need (at scale) and pricing could shift your course to choosing probabilistic data for a campaign's targeting.

THE RISK OF OVERTARGETING

Marketers love to target. Those of us of a certain age were forced to execute mass market programming—such as free-standing inserts and broadcast—for so long that we have been going overboard on digital for more than the last decade. And not overboard on spending. Overboard on *targeting*. Yes, I know, you used to send out a paper coupon in the newspaper to fifty million people on a Sunday—and you're still recovering from that trauma. But that doesn't mean that, in order to have a strong campaign, you need to find Walmart shoppers who live in rural communities, drive a Mazda, have blonde hair, make $50,000 to $75,000, have bought more than three cans of tomato paste but not more than seven cans of tomato paste over the last twenty-six weeks, and have a subscription to at least two lifestyle magazines. Can we find those people? Yeah, we can. But the approach is likely flawed on two accounts: 1) your scale is likely very small, and 2) your costs will be astronomical, with the multiple targeting layers, not to mention the research, that determined that the specific target is all about finding the most likely consumer, not every potential consumer. There's a big difference there.

The scale challenge is straightforward. If there are only 5,000 people who meet this criteria, you aren't going to be making that big an impact across the retailer. Many digital vendors wouldn't even consider executing a program that small.

Second, the fact that the pricing increases with the additional targeting requests brings up the issue of *overtargeting*. What is overtargeting? Knowing that each segment appended to the audience costs $X, at what point do you refine the target so much that it becomes inefficient from a cost standpoint and produces lower GMROIs? Let's say you are marketing a trash bag brand at Target. The category has high household penetration and there isn't a set requirement to be a potential purchaser of trash bags. You aren't going to buy dog food if you don't have a dog. You aren't going to buy baby formula without a baby. But just about anyone needs to buy trash bags. You have worked cross-functionally with your consumer and/or shopper insights teams, and you know that your trash bags sell best with shoppers who live in large suburbs, are thirty-five to fifty-four years of age, have $75K+ household income, and live in households with two-plus kids.

You have found a digital media partner that can serve this target accurately. The cost per thousand impressions (CPM) is $7.50. This accounts for the geographical, age, household income, and household size traits, as well as layering in data relevant to the shopper being a Target shopper (since this is shopper marketing, remember). For the Target designation, the shoppers are using credit card data to show that they are actively shopping the retailer.

Great. Done. Right?

Nope.

The objective of this campaign is to increase incremental sales in the most efficient manner. So, even though your intentions are good, let's hit those most likely to buy our product and encourage them to buy more or increase their trips, because it's easier to increase frequency than to increase household penetration.

The digital vendor comes back to you with this idea:

Let's keep the Target shopper criteria (did I mention it was shopper marketing?) but remove all of the other criteria. As long as they are Target shoppers (remember, almost everyone *could* be a trash bag purchaser), they could get the ad. And the CPM will now only be $3.75

So, we're back to being a mass-reach vehicle. Ugh.

Wait a minute. Could those mass-reach vehicles optimize and get smarter every moment of the campaign? A free-standing insert (FSI) couldn't alter the course of the newspaper deliveries to hit just those people most likely to clip the coupon. But your digital media vendor's platform can.

You are left with a highly targeted approach that's expensive but produces very little waste at any point, or a broadly targeted approach that's inexpensive but will show some inherent waste before optimization takes control and gets you to the right shopper. It boils down to whether that early waste is offset by the fact that the broadly targeted option is 50% of the cost.

Based on my years in the space, the lower-cost, broadly targeted option (as long as it still has the foundational element of being your retailer's shoppers) produces better GMROIs if 1) your brand is in a fairly high household penetration category, and 2) your digital vendor has sound technology and optimization strategies.

In more cases than not, marketers tend to overtarget because they were handcuffed for so long and it's freeing to be able to serve ads to anyone they want. However, we must be aware of those additional costs and the negative impact on the generation of the most optimal GMROI.

TECHNOLOGY

TECHNOLOGY

Other than data, vendors probably are best known for their claims in the realm of technology. You've probably heard comments such as "Our tech is so much better" or "We have a proprietary algorithm that allows us to do this or that." Don't let this ruin your day, because, at the end of it, this might not even matter that much to the success of your shopper marketing campaign. Millions of dollars and man hours go into the engineering of a platform and it *does* matter: the better algorithm, the sturdier pipes, that speediest bidding—all this does, without a doubt, make a difference. There are, however, two issues with that. Number one: the difference it could make could be rendered inconsequential if the platform fails in other pillars that are ranked higher in your Six Pillars Approach outline. Number two: in many cases, the only way to prove the better technology is to test it. To provide some clarification, the technology pillar can include, but is not limited to, the following subjects:

- Platform AI/algorithm/machine-based learning
- Optimization strategy (e.g., moment/impression scoring)
- Cross-device matching accuracy Dynamic creative

optimization (creative decisioning tree limitations)
Connectivity to other platforms
- Location intelligence accuracy (could also be bucketed in the data pillar)

As someone who has been on both sides of the ad tech equation, I have a pretty good idea of the actual impact that a platform's technology can play in performance—and what is simply sizzle. There's a lot of sizzle. But there's also a lot that should simply be table stakes in the market now, and you should be aware of this or it could significantly alter how you interpret an execution's success.

How Does the Platform Optimize?

First and foremost is understanding how the platform optimizes its campaigns. Similar to a lot of areas in this section of the book, I will keep this at a very high level (and that's all that's necessary, to be honest). To begin, under– stand if the campaign is being optimized entirely by the platform and its algorithm, or said another way: is the campaign optimized with machine-based learning? Don't get too worried about how many data points can be analyzed in a millisecond. Chances are that this will have a statistical impact of nada on your actual campaign. It looks good on a slide though. Or is the campaign optimized manually? If so, how frequent is the optimization and how many levers are being pulled: is it simply between audience segments or time of day or device or an entire host of potential factors? Lastly, is it a machine-based optimization with human oversight? This hybrid approach tends to be the most commonly preferred but, in reality, until you test out platforms, there isn't an automatic right and wrong choice. Personally, I tend to trust a machine that can look at thousands of points of data around a single impression in a fraction of an eye blink. And I do this more than any human does—especially a human that's likely managing a dozen other campaigns—but that's me. I have also seen manually optimized campaigns perform wonderfully. Once again, there isn't a concrete right or wrong.

The Importance of Cross-Device Matching

One topic you should never ignore is that of cross-device matching. Accurate cross-device graphs are common– place nowadays. They are, essentially, a prerequisite to do business in the ad tech world. What they bring to the table is no less important in the world of shopper marketing. Ultimately, we want to make sure that the mobile device of user 123 is connected to the desktop device of user 123 as well as the gaming console of user 123. Most importantly, this will allow us, as marketers, to accurately represent a campaign's reach and frequency. This seems to be a no-brainer, but there are still some vendor partners in the marketplace, specifically targeting shopper marketing stakeholders, who don't account for multiple devices. They will count the same person's phone and desktop as belonging to two separate people, and they will tell you they reached a much larger percentage of an audience than they really have.

In addition, this approach can wreak havoc on optimizations. You can serve impressions to a shopper after they converted because the platform can't distinguish between the mobile device and desktop device of the same person. If you recall from the "Deterministic versus Probabilistic" chapter, deterministically addressable data can significantly improve a partner's cross-device graph. Similar to ad fraud and nonhuman traffic issues that plagued marketers in the early 2010s, cross-device concerns are going the way of the dodo. In fact, by the time this book hits stores, you will likely be able to count on one hand your prospective partners who don't have an accurate cross-device solution. That's great news for marketers everywhere!

Personalization versus Relevancy

Dynamic creative optimization, commonly referred to as DCO,

has been around for quite some time. Its impact on shopper marketing has been minimal, but that will likely change over time. DCO is a complex topic—thus, there is an entire section on it—but step one should be under– standing the concept of personalization versus relevancy. In the digital media landscape, as a whole, personal-ization is the rage. But personalization is powered by data, specifi-cally first-party data. In the CPG shopper landscape, we tend to be data poor. But that doesn't mean that we can't strive for ad relevancy using dynamic creative. A car manufacturer might be able to have a single campaign automatically generate 750,000 different versions, based on language, location, income, previous car ownership, previous interaction with ads or site (did you investigate safety features or engine type?), closest dealership, and so on, and coupled with hundreds of thousands of consumers already in the car manu-facturer's massive customer relationship management (CRM) data-base. An organic soup manufacturer trying to sell its item at Albertsons is probably not going to have 750,000 versions. Nor should it. That ad won't say, "Hey Bob, I know you love safety. Here's our latest lane detection capabilities for our model XYZ. Also, here's the closest licensed dealer." But it could showcase the correct Albert-sons logo or populate an address or price point. It could alter the message, based on the weather outside. It could look at your past purchase history or the audience that you belong to and adjust the message For example, if they aren't organic soup shoppers, showcase why organic matters. If they are, highlight a new flavor or benefit that might be different from that of the competitor. If it's the third time they've seen the ad without interacting with it, maybe the benefit changes. We will dive deeper into this in a couple of chapters.

At the end of the day, the technology pillar is going to be higher up in priority on campaigns where performance is more important than finding the right person as outlined by predetermined audience segments, even though it might still nestle into the second or third ranking, as opposed to the first. That's not too shabby!

SEGMENT VERSUS OPEN AUDIENCE TARGETING

One of the biggest debates in performance media is around targeting —specifically, which philosophy to subscribe to: static customer segments or open audience. Like many of the answers to big questions around digital media in shopper marketing, the answer here is that it depends. Both could be the right choice, depending on your primary objective. Before we get into how you should approach this question, let's define these two types of targeting.

Static Customer Segment Targeting

Also known as audience targeting, static customer segment targeting is just what it says it is: targeting a known customer segment or audience. For example, your execution is targeting Kroger shoppers who are twenty-five to fifty-four years of age and buy shampoo. Every single impression, in theory, is being aimed at someone who fits that specific profile. Anyone fifty-five years old or older is out. If the shopper has never bought shampoo, out. If the shopper only shops at Publix, see you later. The positive here is that your media is focusing on what you feel is the primary target of your brand at your retailer.

In shopper marketing, it can also be critical to guarantee that you are serving ads to a person who is a frequent shopper at your particular retailer (or has at least shopped there a few times). You can also expand this where you have multiple static audiences on a buy, and you optimize to the best performing audience. Using the earlier example, one segment could be Kroger shoppers, who are twenty-five to fifty-four years old and buy shampoo, and you could pit that against Kroger shoppers aged eighteen to twenty-four who buy shampoo. The age group that does "better" can receive more impressions as the campaign goes along. This is all pretty straightforward and basic stuff. The negative side of audience targeting is that you are relying on your own data, and your own instincts as a marketer, to really capture the perfect audience segment. You are going to lose out on potential conversions that might fall just outside your target—such as that fifty-five-year-old who desperately wants to buy shampoo at Kroger but needs help deciding which one. You are choosing to rely less on machine-based learning than on open audience targeting, but it doesn't mean you aren't optimizing within the segment to some degree, or optimizing against another segment. Most partners—whether they be a Conversant or a Goodway Group or a Walmart Media Group—utilize this as their base approach. It's the commonest and easiest way for marketers to get behind, maybe because they feel that by choosing the audience segments, they will have some degree of control. They haven't turned the keys over to the robots just yet.

Open Audience Approach

This is a bit more technical and requires two major aspects to put it in the consideration set:

1) you need a partner that has the technological capabilities to execute, and 2) you must be willing to serve ads to consumers who might not be current shoppers at your focus retailer. (Is it okay to rob Peter to pay Paul, if it's only for a few days?) If this is the case, kicking the tires on an open-audience approach may be worth it. The gist of

this philosophy is to remove any major static barriers; it's okay to limit the geo to the USA or say the ads have to go to anyone the age of twenty-one and older, but you shouldn't narrowly focus on a tight demographic or geographic profile. If this is making you cringe, please bear with me. It gets better.

With our shampoo example above, we would now serve ads to all shoppers aged eighteen and older in Kroger geographies (which is almost entirely national), but we aren't saying that they have to be identified as Kroger shoppers (by credit card or location intelligence), and we aren't requiring them to be shampoo purchasers. The ads will start running and, inherently, there will be some waste as the platforms starts understanding the characteristics of those consumers who are engaging with the ad—be it a click, a view, a site visit, or an add-to-cart. Eventually, over time, and depending on how strong the AI of the platform is, you are going to have a more efficient buy because the machine has determined who the right target is by looking at hundreds of thousands of pieces of data on every impression. It may prove your initial target is spot on, or it could show that your previous profile wasn't complete or missed the mark entirely. But you have to trust the machine. Intuitive signals may rise to the top and prove to be influential in determining if someone is likely to perform an action. These secondary and tertiary triggers are likely never in the insight team's playbook. The now defunct Rocket Fuel was one of the first major adtech players to enter this space with their moment scoring mantra and you can see various takes on this at companies such as OwnerIQ and AdTheorent.

I have used and sold tools in both of these camps and neither one was always better than the other. As I mentioned before, it all depends. If you are working on a dog food brand, which necessitates being a dog owner, or trying to sell more coffee pods to owners of Keurig machines, then you should zero in on static audience segments. Even though open audience targeting, if it were doing its job, would eventually reach only dog owners or Keurig households, since they should be the only ones engaging with the ads, the static segments would give you less waste from start to finish. Conversely, if you are supporting a retailer such as Walmart, which is visited by 95% of all Americans, and a product in a category such as toilet paper or cereal, with extremely high household penetration, open audience might be the best route since it can identify intuitive and nonintuitive triggers that go beyond your profile research and improve performance.

As with all of digital media choices, if you have the budgets to do so, test these two approaches against each other on similar campaigns. On paper, one isn't better than the other. They are different and will likely produce a different winner for different brands and different retailers.

DYNAMIC CREATIVE AND THE DEBATE OVER PERSONALIZATION OR RELEVANCY

A great digital shopper marketing colleague of mine, Sameer Badruddin, once told me, "It's not about personal– ization; it's about relevancy." And he was right. We must not fall into the trap of the vast and endless capabilities in digital media (what we *can* do). We should remain grounded in shopper marketing's black and white success metrics (what we *should* do). If we do this, we will see that personalization—though a popular buzzword—is not nearly as important as relevancy when it comes to our shopper marketing ads.

First off, personalization and relevancy are only as good as the data you have collected or can secure from a third party. You can't personalize a message or serve a relevant ad if you know nothing about the shopper the ad is going to. But assuming you have this covered, the differences might seem a bit subtle. Yet they are quite different.

A personalized ad could be a display ad that reads, "Hey, Bob! Celebrate your birthday with the ice cream flavor we know you love. It's available at your local Albertsons on 123 Lettuce Avenue." The shopper's name, the fact that his birthday is coming up, his favorite flavor, and his closest store location would be dynamic personalizations. They would also require a CRM database and/or data management platform to be able to gather and execute against these personal inputs. You might not have this readily available in your shopper marketing team. Depending on your category, your national team might not have this either—at least the known shopper data. For example, if you are manufacturing ice cream, you aren't likely to have a direct-to-consumer business. So, the details of who is actually buying your product at retail is owned by the retailers. You may have data on the shoppers who are engaging with all of your ads, but a click/view/engagement does not equal a sale. In addition, most shoppers tend to find too much personalization a bit creepy, which could negatively impact your business. So, personalization is very challenging in shopper marketing. But that's okay because relevancy is the correct approach.

Relevancy would be making sure you are serving the right ad at the right time to the right person. It's less about showcasing that you know the shoppers' name and birthday and closest store location. It's more about knowing what they need and are looking for in their shopping journey, and delivering a compelling message that influences. So, Bob is having a birthday and is tasked with buying his own decorations and party supplies (poor Bob!). Your digital media vendor might know this because of recent page visitation data or searches. This is more in alignment with his shopping journey as opposed to being tied specially to his birthday. Depending on the data recency, the partner might even be able to look at loyalty card data to see if Bob's already made purchases. If he bought some ice cream a week ago, he might be set and not need an ad served to him. You can also understand that he's an Albertson's shopper by credit card data—and if he's a frequent shopper, there probably isn't a need to use up ad real estate with a small map of his closest store location (Bob knows that already). So we are serving up the right ad (your brand of ice cream in a party atmosphere on the creative), at the right time (around the time Bob's searching other party supplies, but not if he just loaded up on ice cream), and to the right person (Bob). This ad is relevant to Bob without being personalized and freaking him out. Bob doesn't like your knowing where he lives and when his birthday is, Mr. Personalized Banner Ad.

Creative plays a major role in relevancy. DCO can be a pretty powerful tool, but just because it *can* do hundreds of things doesn't mean it makes sense to do them all for shopper marketing. When I was on the vendor side, working for a company with a significant DCO offering, some of the global campaigns would generate 800,000+ versions. Think of all the elements of the ad's creative that could potentially change. The shopper's current location could impact the nearest store (both address and logo), language, and other geo-centric copy ("Y'all" for Dallas, "Yinz" for Pittsburgh). Messaging could be impacted by time of day, the weather, and the shopper's previous interactions with ads: is this the first time the shopper has been served an ad or the ninth time, and what have the shopper's interactions been like? The possibilities are endless. But you don't need endless possibilities in shopper marketing. Here are some simple ways to maximize your shopper marketing campaigns with DCO:

Sequence of, and Engagement with, Ad:
The first time you served an ad, you might want to highlight a benefit (e.g., no added sugar) If the shoppers don't engage with it after you've given it three tries, shift the creative focus to a different variety and highlight the bold flavor . If they do engage with it, you can include a more urgent call-to-action, or a countdown clock creative, calling out a time-sensitive promotion. You can shift the focus from the brand benefit to the retailer to make sure you are driving the sale home to your key customer. This is where it can get really powerful!

Regionally Relevant Copy: This is based on the shopper's geographical location, switching up the copy to be more regionally relevant ("Y'all" versus "Yinz," etc.)

Time of Day: This could be as simple as "Good Morning!" or "Good Afternoon!"

Inventory/Contextual Relevance: If the ad is served on a sports site, it might have sports-centric copy. If it's on a recipe site, it could be about meal planning.

Weather: This would be product category dependent, of course, but offering a message specific to cold weather versus hot weather. The classic example you've probably heard a million times is Starbucks's iced coffee for warm weather, and hot coffee for cold weather. I've also seen it refined for certain products as "Winter isn't here yet, but stock up" and "Winter is here. Go grab our product now."

Banner logos: This is easy, for retailers such as Kroger and Albertsons. They have different store banners (names) in each geography (Kroger in Dallas, King Soopers in Denver, etc.) This allows you to dynamically change them as opposed to assigning media budgets by banner.

To put that in perspective, let's look at two hypothetical rich media/animated banner ads for fictional soda brand Super Fizz. They have a line of both flavor-forward traditional sodas and healthier, all-natural carbonated flavored sodas. You are the shopper marketer for Super Fizz on the Kroger account.

Ad 1: served to a shopper at 4:00 p.m. in Houston, Texas. The weather is sunny and 89 degrees. This is the second ad served to this shopper, who clicked on the first one. We know this is a carbonated soft drink (CSD) shopper, based on our targeting. The ad is served on a desktop when the shopper is on the sports channel ESPN.

What Could This Creative Look Like?

Copy: Good afternoon [determined by time]. We know y'all [determined by geo] love your bold flavors [benefit/attribute focus determined by targeting as well as ad sequence] as much as you love your football [determined by site context and geo], so get your Super Fizz Pineapple Power today at Kroger [determined by geo]. Ten for $10 while supplies last! [determined by ad engagement].

Visual: Brand and Kroger logo; football stadium background

Ad 2: served to a shopper at 9:00 a.m. in Denver, Colorado. The weather is cloudy and 38 degrees. This is the third ad served to this shopper, who has yet to engage. We know this is a sparkling water and craft soda shopper, based on our targeting. The ad is served on a desktop when the shopper is on a news site.

What Could This Creative Look like?

Copy: Good morning [determined by time]! It's cold outside [determined by weather], but staying indoors doesn't mean you have to pack on the pounds [benefit/attribute focus determined by targeting as well as ad sequence]. Drink smarter with Super Fizz all-natural sodas. Nothing artificial [this could be a new attribute to highlight since the first attribute didn't generate an engagement, which was determined by ad engagement]—ever! And that's big news! [determined by site relevance]

Visual: Brand and King Soopers (Kroger) logo; newsroom/newspaper background and graphics

As you can see, the templates for the ad could be identical, but based on numerous elements, the creative would look vastly different and be more relevant to the shopper. This is where shopper marketing needs to go on the DCO front, in the short term, and frankly, it's an underserved area. *You* can change that—and have better ad performance on your campaigns.

E-COMMERCE TECHNOLOGY

No one can deny the importance of e-commerce within the world of CPGs anymore. The COVID-19 pandemic expedited the adoption rate of digitally originated grocery orders fulfilled by delivery or curbside pickup. National ship models also increased, though that system naturally limits categories such as fresh produce and dairy. As of June 2020, with families in quarantine in much of the USA, the household penetration of online grocery increased to nearly a third of all Americans, up from 13% a few months earlier. These targets weren't expected to be met until three to fours years down the road. Even if usage drops postpandemic and the stickiness of online grocery isn't as strong as predicted, e-commerce is still a growing and integral part of the health of your brand at your focus retailer.

The Omnichannel Approach

Despite being the most overused and thrown around word in the world of CPGs, omnichannel *is* the correct approach, as it truly means being representative of "all channels," *not just digitally originated ones.* In-store purchase, as unsexy as it is, still makes up the lion's share of your conversions and is the largest part of the omnichannel equation. But with the laws of physics as we know them today, we can't have a digital ad transport a shopper into a store—and if Gene Roddenberry didn't include it in any of the *Star Trek* series, it will likely never happen. Our digital media buys are left to focus on the e- commerce slice of the omnichannel pie. Don't fret. You know there are a handful of opportunistic vendor partners out there, trying to sell you on capabilities that are "essential" and "critical" to your success in this new world order of grocery shopping. In reality, there *are* some pretty nifty offerings. Though it might now always seem the case, not all vendor partners are bent on stealing your money. We, as shopper marketers, can't let ourselves get caught up in these bright and shiny new objects, even as our bosses are shouting "e-commerce and omnichannel" from the mountain tops at corporate. We have to be diligent and thoughtful and make sure these new tools are moving the needle, driving our business forward at the retailer.

Automatic Add-to-Cart

As it has been for the last few years, when a shopper marketing ad is digitally served, you are likely linking to a product page on a retailer's website. Hopefully, the product page is accurate, with correct descriptions, and has some great enhanced marketing content below-the-fold. When shoppers land on this page, they will have to click again to add it to their cart or list. Simple enough. But can it actually be *more* simple? Firms such as SmartCommerce and MikMak have created the capability to automatically add-to-cart via integrations with some of the biggest retailers in the country. So now, when shoppers click on your ad, your item will automatically be inserted into their cart—and can only be removed if *they* remove it. The hope is that if they were interested enough to engage with the ad, they won't mind it going directly into their cart—and you essentially have saved them a click in what is an extremely frictionless transaction. That's the best-case scenario. Hopefully, you might get some accidental purchases as well, and they will love your product so much that they will keep buying it for years and years to come, right? The importance of getting in a cart or on a list in an online grocery is immeasurable. Per Walmart's e-commerce team in 2018, 50% of their online food and beverage orders were reordered multiple times, once on the shoppers' favorites list. This will only increase in importance as the adoption rate of online ordering increases. What SmartCommerce and MikMak can provide your media executions likely increases those odds of getting in the cart, with or without total shopper buy-in.

I also want to mention that SmartCommerce and MikMak's offerings are tailored for national brand campaigns and brand websites as well. If you have a retailer-agnostic ad running as part of a national campaign, when shoppers engage with the ad, it can bring up an interstitial with different retailer options. The shoppers can choose which retailer cart to add the item to. This, intuitively, should lead to more conversions than simply driving to a product page of one retailer considered to be primary in that particular geo. The same concept can apply to brand websites where a shopper can click on a product and add-to-cart with a litany of retail options.

But does any of this matter? These technologies aren't free and some, in MikMak's case for example, are quite expensive. You are typically paying a monthly fee by brand for unlimited usage, and these costs can range from $12,000 to $80,000 annually, per brand. So, we are left with this simple question: by removing that extra click and automatically adding items to a shopper's cart, do the incremental conversions offset the fees incurred if you use that add-on technology? Or would simply keeping the no-cost approach of directing them to a product page actually be more efficient?

Unfortunately, no one knows the answer. The retailers are still guarding their conversion data, and there isn't any way to track it. A directionally sound A-B test could easily be set up to see the lift of programming with automatic add-to-cart versus ads without. At my most recent employer, we didn't set up strong panels to do a comparison study, but we did have similar campaigns run with and without the technology. The timing wasn't the same and even though it wasn't a seasonal item, that unmatched variable likely rendered our findings irrelevant. Anecdotally, the ads with SmartCommerce *did* drive more conversions, but not enough to offset the costs. We migrated away from the service soon thereafter and saw very little drop-off. Post-COVID-19, however, should be treated as a new landscape, and the lifetime value of the customers who did keep the items in their cart because of the frictionless experience should not be overlooked.

As marketers start to look at these add-ons with more scrutiny, it will interesting to see if these intuitive plus-ups actually are worth the additional costs, or if the vendors change their pricing structure to more accurately reflect the projected impact and not rely on the heightened sensitivity around e-commerce.

MEDIA

MEDIA

The media pillar is the most nebulous, by design. The term *media* is so broad it can mean almost anything and every– thing (or nothing) in our space. However, I've tried to narrow it down to a few key compo- nents that might actually make a difference in your campaign or, at least, should factor into your decision making.

I'm including the following in the media bucket:

- Inventory quality and/or relevance (this may or may not be important at all depending on the campaign objective)
- Inventory safety (this should always be important)
- Available ad formats (types, sizes, native, etc.)

Inventory Quality and/or Relevance

This gets more focus than it probably should. Marketers still go ga-ga over sites they know, routinely visit, or show up on ComScore Top 100 lists. They do this despite the migration to programmatic buying coupled with better data, which gave marketers the ability to shift from focusing on the contextual relevance of a site (which was rife with waste) to the importance of the individual seeing the ad (and, even further, focusing on a particular impression served to that human—when, where, the message, etc.). I get it. We are human. I constantly hear, "Woo hoo, my ad is on ESPN.com—so many eye balls. And I know my brand shopper loves sports." That could be a smart play in some cases, but in reality, you are probably overpaying for the opportunity to be on ESPN.com. If you were selling a plus-up to ESPN subscribers (which you wouldn't, because that's ESPN's job), then this probably would make sense. If you were selling a can of organic soup, wouldn't you want to focus more on people who prefer organic products, shop at your key account, buy a competitive brand, and so on? Yes, they may also go to ESPN.com, but why limit yourself to a premium publisher? And you will waste so many impressions to find that potential organic soup shopper. Then I hear, "But we have a partnership with the [insert the name of the national sports organization] and that's why placing ads on ESPN.com makes sense".

There are a few things to unpack here. If you, as a marketer, believe that the sponsorship with a sports organization will convert people into buying organic soup even if they don't like soup or think organic certifications are just another marketing ploy, then give ESPN all of your money. Please. But even the relevance of a national sports organization and ESPN doesn't remove the fact that you are going to be wasting so much money on shoppers who aren't likely to convert. Leave the wasteful, upper-funnel-awareness, consumer (not shopper) -focused programs to national media organizations. You are a shopper marketer, and you want to drive conversion at your retailer in an effective and efficient manner.

Yes, I'm aware this is a simplified programmatic versus ad network conversation from 2010, but it's good for a baseline of where your head should be, especially if you are newer to digital media. And yes, I also know that you can target organic soup shoppers on premium publishers such as ESPN.com as part of larger buys (or directly, in some cases), but that simply strengthens the notion that it should be about the shopper, not the site's relevance.

With all of that being said, I don't want to come across as saying contextual relevance is entirely pointless. It has its place. For example, if you are can find organic soup shoppers on ESPN and on a grocery-list building site for the same rate (we will get into that in more detail later), I think it's logical to assume that you'd probably side with the grocery-list building site. The likelihood of people being influenced by a compelling organic soup ad when they are making their list (which, if targeting is done correctly, includes the desire to buy organic soup) is higher than when they are checking baseball scores on ESPN. It should be framed as a secondary factor.

The contextual relevance (or lack thereof) of inventory is pretty easy to digest. Inventory quality, as I have named it, is more of a nonmeasurable, nonmetric-based criteria point. As shopper marketers, we typically serve several masters. Sometimes a legitimate but hard to quantify goal is to impress internal stakeholders via a quick two-minute recap or beautifully constructed PowerPoint slide. I am not validating this approach, but it is a reality in many cases where performance isn't paramount. In these cases, sometimes the quality, or more accurately, the *perceived* quality of a site is more important than if it actually moves the business forward.

In a previous role, I was working with a national beverage brand that was handling the shopper marketing efforts for a strategically aligned company. Using the Six Pillars Approach, we had determined that a shoppable recipe network with automatic add-to-cart functionality supporting Walmart's online grocery platform was the proper course of action. The Six Pillars also led us to a preferred partner, Chicory. For those not familiar with Chicory, it is, in very simple terms, a collection of recipe sites where you can place media next to a relevant recipe, or your product can be a shoppable branded ingredient in the recipe. These recipes sites are more along the lines of micro-influencers—they aren't household names or recognizable to the masses—but in aggregate, they represent tens of millions of unique shoppers every month. They are relatively inexpensive, and, for our project, they offered the right attribution. And they had done well on past programs.

But our campaign objective quickly morphed from driving additional usage occasions during a key season (around a holiday) to driving additional usage occasions during a key season (around a holiday) *with a recognizable publisher so that the buyer is happy.*

Enter Allrecipes. I like Allrecipes. I have used them on numerous campaigns, some realizing a ton of success. But for this buy, they didn't fare well in the attribution and pricing pillars. Based on the original objective, media was deemed the most important factor—but with only contextual relevance. Recipe networks jumped to the top of the list, along with longer-form content such as influencer marketing with paid social amplification (recipe blogs that mention our brand, as opposed to being a pairing ad or shoppable ingredient).

Recipe videos were considered, but to compete with recipe networks, they would have to have been served on recipe networks. Attribution was second. So, we ruled out influencer marketing due to its inability, at the time, to capture strong sales data. Based on pricing, video on recipes networks was eliminated because of the higher CPMs, and factoring in the fact that we would have needed to produce videos (and that was way out of our budgetary parameters).

Within that recipe network vendor set, Chicory was more cost-effective than Allrecipes (and others) and had better past performance. It was our choice. Once the objective was revised, media remained the number-one pillar. However, it wasn't just about contextual relevance. It was about *perceived* quality, the is it a household name? test. We never made it to the second pillar—attribution—because only one of our partners within recipe networks hit that pillar subpoint of inventory quality: Allrecipes. So, we ran it. It performed against the goal of making someone happy, but we didn't hit our sales goals at Walmart during that time period. We did, however, win some brownie points from the buyer.

. . .

Inventory Safety

This is more straightforward and should always be part of the campaign discussion. However, over the last few years, very few reputable digital media companies put advertisers in a situation where they have to worry about fraud and nonhuman traffic. It will never be entirely cleaned up, but between the MOATs, DoubleVerifys, IASs, and Peer39s of the world, it's so much better than it was before. This is really me saying that if a prospective vendor mentions an ad verification/safety partner that checks out, you are probably fine moving on to the next pillar of the subpillar. If they look at you funny, kindly ask them to leave the room. Though you don't need to be an expert in all that goes into ad verification to be a strong digital shopper marketer, one point to call out is domain-level versus page-level safety. In simple terms, this is the classic situation in which an airline ad is served on a reputable news site—but on an article about a plane crash. The chance of this happening to your brand is very, very, very small—but it does happen. I worked on a caffeine-rich beverage brand and was made aware of an ad that appeared on an article about a person who went crazy and injured some people—on a caffeine high. No joke. We told the partner that we needed page-level safeguarding moving forward or our relationship would be ending. In their defense, they provided it.

Ad Format

This is something I rarely base a decision on because most vendors support an almost identical roster of sizes and ad types. To be clear, by ad format, I am referring to the sizes and types of ads within a tactical set. For display, the ad formats could include, if they offer them, a 300 x 250 size ad (hint, they do), or animated/HTML5 capabilities (hint, they do), or interactive mobile interstitials (hint, they probably do). I like to bucket rich media in the display/banner bucket, but that, in theory, could be its own tactical set. The same holds true with native ads that take on the creative look and feel of the publisher they live on, as opposed to a fully customizable ad. Granted, some vendors do have uncommon or exclusive formats, be they customized screen takeovers or in-image ads, but these rarely influence a tactic or vendor decision even if there is a curiosity to test performance of the ad format.

ATTRIBUTION

ATTRIBUTION

Attribution is the quite possibly the most misunderstood of the six pillars. Much of the confusion is centered on the various types of attribution across certain verticals—more aptly, the limitations that some industries have when measuring what they define as a success metric. Hint: shopper marketing has some major barriers that have to be overcome, but there are ways to do it.

The Challenge

Let's start with the verticals that have the least resistance and, thus, superior attribution. Retail is probably the best example of the cleanest attribution and has the ability to be the most complex. In the most basic of terms, retailer X knows if shopper A is served media (*most* media, at least; some is still untrackable) and knows if shopper A buys something from that retailer, be it in-store or online. The *how* is not important for this section. By understanding if shopper A was served an email, display ad, video ad, or even TV spots in some cases, and if shopper A came into the brick and mortar location or to the virtual storefront and purchased an item, the retailer can now quantify true return on investment without any modeling. The retailer can also map out which conversion sequences or pathways were the most successful. Maybe after a TV commercial exposure, serving a CRM email, followed by some reminder display ads over the following week, was the most common pathway to conversion. You can assign weighted values on the touchpoint's location in the conversion sequencing (a process referred to a multitouch attribution, among many other names) and decipher which tactics are truly the strongest, most critical performers. Pretty cool, right? Well, don't get used to it, because shopper marketers aren't that lucky.

We have one major issue. The retailer. We can know the shoppers that we served media to, but we lose them at the conversion point because that becomes the property of the retailer—that is, unless you utilize the retailer's own media offering, which we will dedicate an entire chapter to, later on. But fear not shopper marketer! There are ways to measure sales performance with statistical significance without having to be in bed with the retailer.

One assumption I made that is worth clarifying is that the above points really are focusing on sales performance—namely, incremental sales. If you are looking at it from a more digital metric standpoint, or maybe through the lens of a national media or consumer marketing, these statistics are much easier to obtain. As shopper marketers though, it is good to get into the habit of rejecting the correlation between digital engagements such as clicks or video views and actual sales. There is no correlation. You will be engulfed in such metrics on campaign recaps but remember that you care about *one* thing: achieving whatever that shopper objective is.

Metrics

So, which metrics should you focus on? Some common ones are:

- **Incremental sales:** This should be the most common

because it's the only way you are going to know if a campaign hit your ROI benchmark or GMROI benchmark.

- **Incremental New Buyers:** Many brands only care about household penetration and know that they must pay more to obtain a competitive buyer or nonbuyer, so backing into the cost to obtain a new buyer is paramount.
- **Incremental Store Visits/Foot Traffic:** This is most common for certain retailers that don't share their POS data with anyone. The biggest example would be the convenience store class of trade. Though a flawed metric, it still outpaces metrics such as clicks or impressions in relevancy.

You need a strong GMROI, right? How do you measure that? First, you need to understand the *incremental* sales that can be *accurately* attributed to the campaign.

Gross Margin Return on Investment ("GMROI")

$$\text{GMROI} = \frac{\text{Incremental Profit}}{\text{Media Spend}}$$

One Major Callout

Please don't fall for retailers and vendors that share ad attributed or media influenced sales. This calculation of return on ad spend (ROAS) does not capture the actual incremental impact.

Return on Ad Spend ("ROAS")

$$\text{ROAS} = \frac{\text{Revenue Attributed to Media*}}{\text{Media Spend}}$$

*does not factor in incrementality

All that is saying is that people saw the ad and bought something. This ignores the fact that they might have bought it anyway. In other words, the campaign was set up without a test versus control mechanism. Take shopper A and shopper B. They are virtually identical. Shopper A is served the ad; shopper B is not. Shopper A purchases; shopper B does not. This means that the sale to shopper A was, indeed, incremental, and the media buy should get credit for that sale. Once you know the incremental sales (and your profit margin), you can compare that to your spend and produce your GMROI for the program.

There are three ways to understand incremental sales of a program: two are entirely restricted to the retailer media networks' walled gardens of data. One can be used across most digital partners. All three can be statistically significant.

User-level matching is when the test and control panels are made up of nearly identical shoppers, similar to the example above with shopper A and shopper B. This granular data can be derived from sources such as loyalty cards or online profiles. Kroger knows me by my loyalty card number and knows my purchase history at its stores. It can find someone almost identical to me in location, age, and anything that is on the form that I used to sign up for the card. More importantly, it can match my purchase history to someone very similar to me. This user-level match is commonly regarded as the most complete and accurate since it's at the individual level.

Household-level matching follows the same methodology, but the matching is done at the household level. A retailer such as Walmart doesn't have my individual information (unless I'm shopping Walmart.com) but does have receipt data from my in-store purchases. Partnering with companies such as Experian and

Walmart can take that receipt data and match the credit card I used to a household.

Understandably, there is some drop-off in the matching, and it doesn't include shoppers who pay with cash. However, scale is not an issue when you are talking about the volume of information from a retailer such as Walmart.

Store-level matching is the most frequently used methodology. Though it's not as accurate as user- or household-level matching, most campaigns of adequate size hit a minimum of 85% statistical significance, which should pass muster with even the most critical of analytics teams and data scientists. In addition, store-level matching can be done through a variety of partners and doesn't force a shopper marketer to funnel budgets to retailer media networks just to get an accurate performance metric.

Store-level matching consists of setting up test and control stores within a single retailer that are similar in location, shopper demographics, all commodities volume (ACV), category and brand sales (of the item being advertised). If done properly, pricing (since the individual matches are in same retailer and same geography) and national media and promotions (same geography) should affect the test and control stores equally. Therefore, the only difference between the stores is the presence of your digital media campaign. The one component that cannot be accounted for is any store-specific programming or issues. For example, the test store has some merchandising that went up, but it was taken down in the control store. Some of these outliers can even be removed postanalysis. This has been an accepted measurement methodology for in- store programming for decades, and in digital media since 2013. Companies that offer services such as this include Retail Solutions, Inc. (RSi)—offering its Ansa tool—IRi, Pathformance, and others.

. . .

You may be more familiar with national incremental sales attribution vendors such as Datalogix or the former Nielsen Catalina Solutions, but these are more national, using a blinded roster of retailers to model out the total US impact of your campaign. They are not meant for single-retailer shopper marketing programs.

IN-FLIGHT SALES OPTIMIZATION

Almost every program you will ever run will have some sort of in-flight optimization. The inputs fueling that optimization can be vast and variable (time of day, browser, recent site visits, geo, etc.), but the performance metric that the program is optimizing should be singular and firm (incremental sales, completed video views, sign-ups, etc.). In most cases, we are going to optimize on a sales metrics since we are shopper marketing, after all.

If you've talked to digital media vendors in the past, then you know they have all claimed to have in-flight sales optimization. They aren't lying, but they also aren't telling you the truth as it pertains to your unique shopper marketing needs—that is, you are only concerned with sales at a single retailer. The in-flight optimization that they speak of, made famous by Nielsen Catalina Solutions (NCS) taps into a blinded network of retailers to optimize; it can't be broken out by a single customer nor does it include some major players such as Walmart, Kroger, and Target. These programs usually come with a national media-level budget (in the hundreds of thousands of dollars). So, it's fine that they only make sense for national media executions.

That leaves digital media vendors with only a handful of options when it comes to account-specific sales attribution on a shopper marketing budget. RSi, Information Resources, Inc. (IRi), and Path-formance are three qualified attribution partners that can give you account-specific POS data to produce an incremental sales total using test-control methodology. But since they don't have first-party customer data from the retailer, you are measuring on a store-level match (as discussed in the previous section). As long as you reach your acceptable level of statistical significance, that shouldn't matter. But what about optimizing in-flight (that's the name of this section, isn't it?)? What RSi pioneered back in 2013 was the ability to take the real-time flow of POS data and use it to shift where impressions are served. So, using your store-matched test-control, if you see 100 Walmarts are generating the most incremental sales, maybe you shift impressions in-flight to those stores. Conversely, if there are some stores that aren't responding to the ads, remove them from the buy. At the end of the day, you will be focusing your media investment on the stores that are driving more incremental sales and making the most positive contribution against your GMROI goal.

On the topic of incremental sales, as you run these campaigns, make sure that the vendor partner understands that your focus is total incremental sales and not incremental sales *lift*. It can totally change the outcome of a program if the platform optimizes against lift and not raw incremental sales. As you know, a 10% incremental sales lift on Campbell's soup means something totally different from a 10% lift on ReaLemon. One could mean millions of dollars; the other could mean a few thousand, all determined by the base volume of the brand being measured. If you look at it on the store level, you don't want the platform to optimize to stores that are showing a higher lift, because it could be a component of a lower baseline and just selling a few more items. If your overall campaign goal is to generate the most efficient GMROI, sales lift could leave you with a great lift percentage and a terrible GMROI. But you know the vendor is going to be hyping that double-digit lift percentage!

If you optimize total incremental sales, your impressions will go to the stores generating the *most* incremental sales, whether it's against a large or small baseline. The more incremental sales you generate, the more profit and the better GMROI you'll get. It's as simple as that. Unfortunately, driving GMROI is harder than lift. And most vendor partners, in conjunction with the attribution partners, default to lift so they can always share good news. Be cognizant of this and adjust accordingly!

PRICING

PRICING

One key lesson from my years in the digital media space that rings true time and time again is that you get what you pay for. Having spent a large portion of my career on the vendor side, I can honestly say that they are going to get their cut, no matter what. If you, as a shopper marketer, get a too-good-to-be-true rate, it probably is. Your ad will either have very loose targeting or you will end up on some undesirable inventory. The vendor will save on data fees or media fees to make sure it keeps the lights on. So, what is the right price? That's an unanswerable question, unfortunately. But before you use price as a determining factor in choosing a vendor, remember to understand where that pillar fits in your ranking. If your objective is about hitting a certain target, no matter the cost, and you have two vendor options that meet that criteria, then price could be the tiebreaker. If you're worried about delivering on an ROI benchmark, it's likely an important factor as well, considering that the efficiency of your spend will be the denominator in your ROI equation. But the technology could also drive better performance, even if the pricing is higher. This is why the right price doesn't exist. You must test to under– stand the balance between price and the other pillars.

However, really think about where price is weighted among the six pillars so that you won't be star-struck by a really low rate or remove a vendor or tactic from consideration due to sticker shock.

In my experience, when you have two or more vendor options that have extremely similar offerings, data sources, attribution partners or methodologies, and inventory sources—and you don't have any past campaigns to compare them with—price is likely the deciding factor. However, if the gap between vendor A and vendor B is wide, make sure to investigate before signing the contract. They could be hiding something or they could simply be willing to eat some profit to win your business. Just be smart and aware.

PAST PERFORMANCE

PAST PERFORMANCE

To be honest, when your past campaign repository becomes so robust that it can jump to the top of your Six Pillars Approach, you are in a really good place! Though this is self-explanatory, I do have a few callouts to watch out for when comparing programs.

No Final Verdict from One Campaign

One campaign result shouldn't be a final verdict. As much as we want to give everyone our money or cut

someone from the consideration set, based on one test, don't. Even in the best of times, your best performer isn't going to perform to your benchmarks every single time. After a few tests, you will see trends develop, and then it's up to you to slice and dice those results further, because ...

... retailers, classes of trade, brands, categories, and messages matter.

Especially if you are a company representing different brands, or if your shopper responsibilities cover multiple retailers or classes of trade, it's recommended to test as much as your budgets will allow. The same vendor and tactic could show radically different results for a coffee brand at Kroger, targeting millennials with an emotionally charged message about ethical sourcing versus a soda brand advertising a price promotion to large families at Dollar General. It could be that the vendor's targeting, inventory, or technology is just better suited for millennials or shoppers of grocery stores, or it could be some poor optimizations by a campaign manager, or it could be that the program really had little chance for success. Net net, that vendor shouldn't be given all of your business, or entirely cut, based on a mixed bag of results.

In my past lives, I have tried to bucket tactics and vendors by KPIs first, and then by brand and/or category, and then by retailer and/or class of trade. A vendor that would never be considered for driving incremental sales at a grocery retailer might be my go-to for driving incremental store visits at a convenience chain.

Customer Service

It often gets overlooked when considering a potential vendor but it shouldn't. Customer service should factor into performance. If vendor A averages a $1.25 GMROI and vendor B averages a $1.10 GMROI—both eclipsing your internal benchmarks—but vendor A adds hours upon hours of work on your plate with poor communication, constant errors that you have to correct prelaunch, slow response times, and a general lack of shopper marketing knowledge, then you need to decide if that extra $0.15 on every $1 in profit is worth it, because it could keep you from focusing on another aspect of your business. And that could have a negative financial impact well beyond that $0.15. Only you can make this call.

In such a crowded space as digital media, no vendor should be providing sub-par customer service.

Conversely, if a vendor has been given multiple chances to

perform and has failed every time but is really, really nice and smart and helpful, it still is time to cut bait. Wish that vendor well and suggest switching to one of those vendors that has a great product but horrible representation!

DIGITAL MEDIA TOOLS IN A SHOPPER MARKETING WORLD

THE RISE OF RETAILER MEDIA
NETWORKS

The most sensitive obstacle shopper marketers face, specific to digital marketing, is the rise of retailer-owned platforms, commonly referred to as retailer media networks. These networks place shopper marketers in a unique and precarious position where they have to potentially pit tangible sales performance versus the more nebulous return on relationship. To understand why you could be at this proverbial fork in the road, it's good to understand the role of retailer media networks.

Data You Can't Live Without

As their margins continue to shrink, retailers have scrambled to find additional sources of revenue—and they've discovered that one of their most precious resources is their data. Not only do they know who you are, based on your online or loyalty card profile, but they know what you're buying—and what you're not buying, from those same loyalty cards or a combination of receipt and credit card data. This first party data is highly sought after, and it should be to no one's surprise that nearly every major grocery, mass, drug, and convenience retailer has built impenetrable walled gardens around this coveted resource.

This isn't without precedence in the digital world—hello, Facebook and Google—and it's not, in and of itself, a bad thing. The data is great—quite possibly the best for a shopper marketer—but you will find that what they've built around the data and how to access it leaves a lot of be desired.

The retailers knew that shopper marketers' mouths were watering at the opportunity to build audiences for their brands with actual purchase-based data from their focus retailer. It's the perfect scenario. Right out of the gate, their attempts to monetize were clunky at best, some choosing to sign on selling agents, such as Triad and Quotient, that had reputations within the industry that left a lot to be desired. Others tried to build it internally with talent that lacked real digital knowledge, be it Target Media Network (now Roundel) or Kroger and its in-house data goliath, 84.51. In all cases, they adopted the model of "Hey, marketer, you *have* to run with us so take whatever I give you and like it." They approached the business with no strategic vision, nor did they really care to be a good steward for their suppliers' brands. It was about the money. The severity of this charge varied by retailer. In the worst cases, you were given vendor income targets to hit: you had to spend X dollars with the retailer or you would be delisted, deprioritized, or worse. These amounted to digital slotting fees. And we shopper marketers (along with our sales and trade counterparts) paid it. More subtle approaches included restricting the usage of the retailer logo on third party media, and trying to route marketers' budgets back to the retailer platform. *You run with us, or you don't run anything at all.*

Once again, they would rather your brand struggle and fail than succeed without cutting them checks for their digital offerings.

However, the most frustrating part of this meteoric rise of retailer media networks is simply the fact that all of this tension and contempt could have been avoided. As I mentioned before, the first party data that they had access to is best in breed. But the tech stack around the data was never a focus. Great data can be quickly relegated to worthless data if the technology around it is suspect, such as the lack of a functioning cross-device graph (Target), the inability to optimize in-flight based on sales data (essentially all retailers), and even the inability to utilize real-time look-alike modeling/propensity targeting (all but Walmart).

A Price Only a Mother Could Love

The other thing that can kill the effectiveness of great data is pricing. This was a profit center for the retailers, which is most apparent in their pricing strategies. Inventory is routinely priced three to four times that of open market value. Even premium onsite placements (on the retailer's own site) outpaced the most premium inventory on top publishers. When your goal is to drive incremental sales in an efficient manner, as it is with most shopper marketing objectives, a $20 CPM is going to make that nearly impossible, especially for a can of soup or a bag of chips or two liters of diet soda. On top of technology deficiencies and outrageous pricing, the retailers (or more likely, their selling agents) levied ridiculous rules and restrictions around their products. For Albertsons, Quotient Technology forced a minimum spend of $250,000 to get statistically significant incremental sales testing, knowing that very few shopper teams had the ability to spend a quarter of a million dollars on a single Albertsons campaign. Target and Kroger issued similar measurement minimums. Sam's Club's online media programs (OMPs) capped the amount of behavioral (purchase-based) or keyword-based targeting that a brand could utilize on a single campaign. Kroger Precision Marketing mandated that at least 50% of your target audience had to be made up of existing brand buyers. So, household penetration objectives were immediately handicapped. The retailers took their most desired asset (first party data), watered it down with bad technology, priced it beyond the realm of acceptability, and added self-serving, one-sided restrictions so that any glimmer of hope that the program would grow your brand in an efficient manner was soundly squashed.

But What Can You Do?

That's why retailer offerings are challenging and likely aren't right for your brand. What can you do? The most crucial step is understanding what you are getting for your participation and what would truly be lost if you spent less (or none) of your current budget with the retailer. Retailers prey on fear. However, what retailers fail to realize is that more effective third-party digital campaigns can offset any potential business loss that could materialize from your merchant's threats (assuming that they go through with them). If hitting a certain spend level with a retailer gets you some seasonal limited time offers (LTO) that you feel will net you millions in top line sales, then you likely will choose to participate. If your answer is "It's good for the relationship," I would spend time trying to quantify that before you willingly sign that retailer media network insertion order. If there is a time to test what truly will improve your business, it's in the head-to-head bakeoffs between a retailer platform and a third-party execution. This was one of my main priorities at a Fortune 500 CPG that I worked for. This CPG had almost always followed orders from the retailer. For one of the CPG's top brands, I set up a head-to-head test between a key retailer's platform and one of our preferred third-party media partners. Both executions were test/control and both ended up with over 95% statistical significance. The fact that the third party outperformed the retailer offering shocked no one, but the fact that it generated a gross margin ROI that was thirteen times stronger opened some eyes. We quantified the lost incremental, top-line sales at well over $1,000,000 for this eight week period, and need– less to say, the positive return on relationship would not have generated that much in that given time period. The results were validated over the course of dozens of tests. Third-party executions produced gross margin ROIs of five to six times that of a retailer media network buy. Your results may vary, depending on your brands, retailers, choice of third-party media partner, and so on, but in my history of dealing with these platforms, it holds true.

What is the future of retailer media networks? Chances are that they will continue to be an integral part of your digital strategy, whether that is to include them or remove them from the consideration set. In a cheerier and more optimistic future, the retailers will see the error of their ways and try and make these platforms more effective for their brands. They will charge less but generate more actual sales in their stores (both physical and virtual). They will focus on why their programs aren't working beyond pricing, sharpening their technology to the point that would rival the most powerful ad tech giants in the space. They will listen more to the shopper marketers who have decided to shift money away from them, and less to their selling agents who are using the name of the retailer to force advertisers with tactics of fear and misdirection. Or they could continue down the path of "You have to spend with me or else" and start to enforce the "or else" in a more tyrannical and oppressive manner. I have faith in the retailers. As the shopper marketing community becomes more savvy and pushes on the inadequacies of their offerings, they will evolve. That will be a great day for all.

DEVELOPING A RETAILER PAID SEARCH PLAN

We already talked in detail about retailer media networks but the focus there was more on their digital *media* offerings" display, video, and so on. One tool they also offer that should be reviewed separately is retailer paid search, also known as onsite search. Less than a year ago, when click and collect/curbside pickup models were still trying to gain a foothold, onsite search seemed to focus more on items that could easily be nationally shipped profitably, such as coffee makers on Walmart.com, or potato-chip variety packs on Amazon.com, or razors at SamsClub.com. Items that were low margin—where you *could* ship, but those costs made them undesirable and were made worse if the items were heavy—didn't have to play in onsite search because it was all about getting consumers in the store. Media was the right play for such items, and onsite search was strictly for those e-commerce-focused brands such as the coffee makers, potato-chip variety packs, and razors mentioned earlier. Now with the omnichannel world that we live in, and adoption rates for online grocery pickup and delivery skyrocketing, your brand has the ability —and some say a necessity—to "win" the digital shelf and make sure your product is front-and- center. But how does a shopper marketer do that exactly?

First, let's look at the importance of onsite search. As far back as 2015, studies have concluded that 67% of shoppers start at the retailer site—not with a national search engine such as Google. This makes sense. In fact, Amazon and Walmart are now among the top five search engines.

When you conduct a search on a retailer's site, the results will be a mix of organic and paid placements. The organic placements are driven by the retailer's algorithm, which is proprietary but is likely made up of inputs such as top sellers, most profitable items, relevancy, and how well the product page is keyword optimized. The only one that you, as a shopper marketer, can actively control is the keyword optimization of your product page. The retailers have an opinion on what they want to sell, all things being equal, and that will dictate organic placement more than anything. But you can impact the paid placements. And these placements are only increasing as retailers are seeing them as an even more profitable monetization point than controlling the organic rankings. Each retailer platform has a different number of spots and placement locations that are designated for paid ads. Understanding the right interplay between organic and paid is difficult but critical. What does jumping up one spot in the rankings do to your sales?

Why does this matter? Ninety percent of conversions occur from placements in the top three rows. So yeah, that's why it matters. But is it worth paying a lot money for? Or should the focus be on the slower organic build?

As we look at the platforms, all retailers have their unique set-ups with pros and cons. The landscape itself is vastly different than it was a few years ago. Before, you could get by with some spend on Amazon and an aggregator network such as Criteo. Now, with more focus on digital conversions and each account putting more pressure on brands to spend with their platform (see "The Rise of Retailer Media Networks" section), you will need to be wired in to a dozen or two distinct platforms. It's not just Walmart and Kroger; Hy-Vee, Wakefern, Boxed, and Ahold all have ways to purchase paid search placements.

To keep your sanity, it's best to boil it down to the most mission-critical aspects.

- Should we test the platform?
- Does it work?
- How can we make it work better?

Each one is progressive. So, if it doesn't pass step 1, don't proceed to step 2.

Should We Test the Platform?

As I stated before, platforms come in all shapes and sizes. Here are some characteristics that you are surely to be inundated with as you research options:

- Natively built, or third party: this is the platform built by the retailers themselves (Walmart grocery), or are the retailers tapping into a third party (e.g., Albertsons utilizing Quotient)?
- Placements and ad types: where are the paid/sponsored ads served? For example, Amazon reserves the first, second and third spots for paid; Kroger reserves the fifth, seventh, and ninth. And are there other placements across the site—for example, Kroger's Start My Cart page or Sam's Club's keyword-triggered display ads.
- Bid management and optimization: what are the opportunities and limitations in controlling bids and the optimization of a campaign? As an example, Hy-Vee requires all bid and optimization strategies to pass through a review process, which slows down the ability to

jump on trends in real-time, thus, negatively impacting the performance.

- Reporting and measurement: How timely and customizable are the reporting capabilities? Are you getting real-time and customizable reports? Are you getting in-flight customer insights? Are you getting a dashboard with an intuitive UI?

Guess what? These are all great, but *none of them* should be the reason you decide to run or not run with a platform.

Your decision to invest in a platform should come down to three easy questions (with two having mild caveats):

- **Is this a "tier 1" retailer?** (You can define what tier 1 means.) It could be. Does it meet a certain threshold of sales per month and does it have accurate product images and descriptions. I don't care if a new personal shopper service has the best platform and reporting in the world. If you're selling $50,000 annually there and your product images are from three years ago, likely pulled off Google Images, there's no need to invest in it right now.
- **Is it a self-service platform?** If you can't control your budgets and bids, walk away. Your program will not be optimized properly. The caveat here is that if your organization doesn't have a search specialist to pull the levers and you don't have the time to, then, maybe, don't write off the platform entirely.
- **Can you bid at the keyword/search term level?** If you are stuck at the category level, it could be too broad and inefficient. For example, if you are an orange juice brand and can only bid at the juice category level ,then you will be bidding against, and showing up among, cranberry juice, lemon juice, tomato juice, and so on. This is not ideal. The two caveats here are that 1) it's

totally fine for some products to remain at that category level, and 2) platforms define categories differently. Some are broader, while others are pretty specific (which is great).

Does It Work?

One of the most frustrating aspects of dealing with onsite search is the bastardization and blatant misrepresentation of results. ROAS this, ROAS that. These are all ad/media-attributed sales. The platform is getting credit for *every* sale on a sponsored ad regardless of whether it was going to happen or not. For example, if shoppers search "cereal" and Fruit Loops pops up first, they click on it, add it to their cart, and buy it. Great. But those users buy Fruit Loops every single week. That sale was going to happen if you were in placement 1 or placement 11. A positive ROAS will be showcased, but it's not incremental, and that investment should be considered a loss.

The question Does it work? is harder to figure out due to the complexity of search versus more straightforward media such as targeted display ads or in-store signage. With that media, you can create test and control panels—be it at the user, household, or store level—to help determine incrementality. Search doesn't have a static characteristic to use as a control since you can't dictate the audience or geo or store you are going to be serving your ad to. It makes it really messy. I won't pretend to have an answer as I simply don't have the data science and statistics chops to create a test design with confidence, but from past experience, using time as the foundation for the control versus test has produced directional data that seemed to work.

That would simply be executing a search program at a certain budget for a week, off a week, on a week, off a week (it doesn't have to be a week interval) and understanding the delta in your total sales between the weeks with support and weeks without it.

A few major watch-outs:

- The buys must not cross major marketing investments as you want both national and shopper marketing media investments to impact each week in the same manner.
- The standard incremental calculation of *net relative % sales change* cannot be utilized here because the base period (e.g., the previous weekly average for fifty-two weeks) would apply exactly the same to the test and control panels (since the panels are arbitrary time periods and not users/households/stores).
- Use only nonbranded keywords/search terms.
- Sales bleed will need to be considered (sales influenced by the campaign but the conversion fell outside the measurement period).

This test design is also taking a big leap of faith that each week-long execution will use roughly the same bid amounts, keywords, and so on. The granular optimizations and strategies are critical, but they should be held until step 3. If, after a few executions across a platform, every program directionally does not pay out, you should abandon paid search on that particular platform and focus simply on improving organic to the best of your ability (i.e., optimize your product pages, try and drive total sales of your brand through media and marketing and hope that total sales of the brand is a key component in the retailer's algorithm).

How Can We Make It Work Better?

Once you deem the platform to be potentially viable at producing a positive return, the goal should be to set up brand or category-level playbooks. These will help outline how to make search campaigns work even better over time. Let's say that you are a laundry detergent company with multiple brands that fit different needs: brand A for the general population, brand B for value shoppers, and brand C for premium and all-natural shoppers. Walmart.com's search platform has met all of your criteria (tier 1, self-service, and keyword-targeted) and you've proven that it is producing strong GMROIs. So, step 1 and 2 are done. Now, it's time to fine-tune your programming via a playbook. But why?

Brand and SKU Prioritization

Think about this. For the term *laundry detergent*, what brand should "win"? The general population detergent, due to its mass appeal? Brand B because it speaks more to the Walmart shopper? Brand C because its margins are better? That's for you to decide, but you have to make a call and test it out. You might think it's brand A, but after significant testing, you could realize it's brand B. For the sake of this exercise, I will take three search terms and assign them a brand: laundry detergent is brand A, cheap detergent is brand B, and natural detergent is brand C. There are likely hundreds of terms that need to be assigned, but using only three will keep it simple. So, for laundry detergent, you have brand A, but which stock keeping unit (SKU)? Do you want to highlight the liquid or the pods? What size and what count? This is where you can make the call to go with higher volume SKUs since they are the most popular and recognizable to the consumer, or the most profitable SKUs and try and influence shoppers to trade up to those sizes that yield the most profit. Both are sound approaches. As you can see, this can get extremely complex.

Category and Brand Optimization Strategies

This portion of your playbook includes your classic lever-pulling. Your search analyst should feel right at home here. This is where you can help outline the impact of departing, value of higher/lower costs per click, when to conquest, and so on, by brand and category, and don't forget, by platform. What works on Amazon may or may not work on Walmart.

. . .

Category and Brand Insights

If the category and brand optimization strategies are what is learned intracampaign, insights are postcampaign. They would include broader learnings after a campaign has been executed in full. You are limited to what the platform provides, but it could include information such as demographics, new buyer percentage, and items of that ilk. You would use what has been learned to influence future buys on that platform for those brands/categories. Once again, these insights should be specific to the platform.

The goal with search is simple: make sure it's the right platform for your brand to invest in, prove that it is actually driving incrementally, and if it is, build playbooks to consistently improve your campaigns by assigning the appropriate brands and SKUs to keywords and leveraging intra- and postcampaign learnings.

FIRST SCAN OPTIMIZATION

One of the more challenging aspects in the CPG goods world is to successfully introduce new products into the marketplace. Aside from the more pressing issues such as getting shelf space and generating ample awareness nationally, shopper marketers are tasked with parlaying the national spends with programming that can alert a retailer's shoppers that the new product is available at said retailer. It can be a tricky situation because, unlike their national counterparts, shopper marketers' budgets don't allow for wasteful spending on spray-and-pray media. We all know new products are cut into stores at different times—if at all. This forces shopper marketers to wait until critical mass is reached before media is turned on, or even worse, guess when critical mass will be reached.

Digital media does provide a solution beyond the ability to be turned on more quickly than traditional shopper marketing tools such as in-store signage with its ridiculously long lead times. It can go one step beyond being extremely turnkey. A brand can eliminate 100% of the waste by using POS access via partners such as RSi to turn on digital media around stores the day after the product scans.

Many detractors will claim that it will be difficult for this type of execution to pay out and that there is a reason to wait until adequate distribution before supporting with marketing. They aren't wrong. Though even at that juncture, payout on a new product innovation will be an uphill battle. Two things to consider: 1) should the primary KPI for a new launch be something other than GMROI, and 2) if it takes two to three months to get to what is defined as "adequate" store coverage, can a new product survive a period that long with no retailer-specific support, especially in it's pivotal introductory phase? The answers are yes and no, respectively.

By turning on digital ads around stores, post first scan, the program is likely to overspend on those earlier stores— but if broken down on a spend per day, it should be relatively consistent. Those are simple guard rails that any media vendor executing a first-scan buy can implement. Then again, even if there were some overspend around a select number of stores, that would still be preferable over spending dollars for a store that didn't even have the item in stock.

So, what should the KPI on a new product launch be? For the overall launch, the objective is likely awareness and, subsequently, trial generation. For the digital first scan execution, it's a bit murkier but, ultimately, it comes down to velocity. An argument can be made that the real goal is the elimination of waste during the all-important nascent phase of a product, and that every impression served around a store with the product actually in it is, technically, a success. With that being said, it's always a good idea to measure incrementally, even if it's not the judge, jury, and executioner for the program. Over time, as you launch more and more products, a benchmark can be established on what a reasonable GMROI is for product innovation. If you require a $1.00 GMROI for a standard shopper marketing campaign to be deemed a success, maybe be it's $0.40 for innovation. Maybe it's $0.75. Heck, maybe it's $0.10. As with all tactics, the more testing and business outcomes you can generate, the better opportunity you will have to optimize future recommendations and executions.

DIGITAL VIDEO AS A SALES DRIVER

Ever since I ran my first shopper marketing digital media campaign in 2013, I've heard from everyone that video doesn't make sense for shopper marketing. It's too expensive! It's too much to produce! Video ads are just annoying! It seemed as if the naysayers controlled the narrative for a long time, but I'm happy to say that the story of shopper marketing video is far from over.

First things first: I will mostly be referring to in-stream video ads, and the majority of those ads are pre- and midroll. Yes, postroll video ads do exist, but it's likely a fraction of your spend (if anything at all). I also know that in-banner and outstream video are also utilized by brands. Admittedly, in my own journey, I have relegated both of these formats to second-tier status because they are not part of the captive video viewing experience. Does this mean that they don't work? Not necessarily. But if the goal is to validate that video ads can drive incremental sales of a brand at a specific retailer in an efficient manner (thus, producing a respectable GMROI), then the focus should be on the truest form of video ad. The inventory source is where we will delineate within the world of video.

One of the reasons that video was thrown out of the universal consideration set was that it was too expensive, especially when compared to the average CPMs of banner ads. A lot of things have changed since the onset of digital media, one of those being that inventory for videos has skyrocketed, so rates have lessened. You are still going to pay three to four times that of a display ad. However, in certain circumstances, performance of video should outpace display by an even greater clip. That is really step one in determining if video works for your campaign: understanding what *type* of message you're trying to convey. For example, if your brand is launching a new flavor —Blackberry Watermelon Jamboree—then a simple banner ad will likely be sufficient to get that message across. A shopper probably doesn't need long-form content to explain what blackberries and watermelons are; the brand probably doesn't need a medium such as video, with sound and motion and a story, to tug on the heartstrings of shoppers in order to get them motivated to buy this new extension. A video campaign showcasing this new flavor *could* outperform a banner ad execution, but is it going to outperform it by such a margin as to offset the premium costs of the video ad? Not likely. Over time, working across multiple verticals, a handful of message types have aligned nicely with video execution and generating lower funnel conversions in an efficient manner.

- **Complex messages:** for example, trying to explain why a new ingredient has potentially positive effects on digestion.
- **Emotional connection:** for example, showcasing acts of kindness that emphasize
- the brand's commitment to social responsibility in the retailer's geographical footprint.
- **Product demonstration:** for example, walking through the easy four-step process of a new home appliance.
- **Alternative usage occasions or appetite appeal:** for example, letting shoppers know that a soda

brand is also perfect for baking, mixing cocktails, and drinking on a hot summer day.

- **Recipes in action:** for example, using video to really highlight the appetite appeal of a dish of which the featured brand is an integral ingredient—and an opportunity to pair it with your customer's private-label products.
- **Generate excitement with the retailer merchant/buyer:** Sometimes, video comes across as if the brand were making a bigger commitment than other digital tactics (and rightfully so) and because of this, generates a bit more excitement with the buyers. They tend to feel that if a brand is going to utilize custom video, then the supplier is really getting behind this campaign. This shared excitement could lead to additional in-store merchandising and support from the customer.

For the above types of message, a simple banner ad won't likely cut it. Can you imagine trying to explain the health impact of a reformulation of a product in a 300 x 250 rectangle? Or establishing a personal connection with a shopper about how the brand gives back to struggling farms in impoverished countries on a 300 x 50 mobile ad? It would be beyond challenging. Video gives you a better chance to communicate this type of message in a meaningful way—and outpace the cheaper, higher-volume tactics such as digital displays. But that's not the only factor to consider. Not only are CPMs higher for video, the production costs are likely much, much higher. Spending too much on a nonworking aspect of a campaign is a sure fire way to destroy any chance for a positive GMROI.

Overcoming the very real hurdle of production costs can be time-consuming and will add a bit of additional work for you and/or your creative agency. However, it can be done. As a rule of thumb, it's best to try and keep the percentage of your spend that's nonworking/production-related to 10% or lower, give or take. Every percentage point above that will make it that much harder to generate a solid GMROI and validate the decision that video was the right tactic. If the budget for your campaign is $75,000, the target for production should be $7,500. That seems a big ask to produce a quality video asset for that limited amount. But I'll reiterate: it can be done. Here are some things to consider.

- **Don't rely on your agency:** In my experience, an agency partner is never going to be as scrappy as someone at the client company. It doesn't directly behoove them to be, as much as they might claim to be doing what's best for your brand. I'm not suggesting that you don't give them an opportunity to find a cost-effective solution, but don't assume they are coming to you with the best option.
- **Don't compare the video asset to that of a studio-produced commercial:** It's not going to be a Super Bowl ad, so stop thinking it will! And that's not a bad thing. One prevailing opinion is that the cleaner, overproduced commercials tend to be overlooked or negatively thought of (especially in social platforms) more than lower-budget, guerrilla-style creative, especially when they are authentic and compelling.
- **Do consider simply tagging a national asset:** This is the cheapest and easiest approach, though it might not be the best (even if it's essentially free). If your national team has produced a video ad that you feel would translate as a lower-funnel message, then adding on an intro/end card that showcases the retailer could be enough to make it a viable shopper marketing creative. The obvious callout is that the retailer is simply an afterthought, thus negatively impacting the amount of conversions at said retailer. However, that waste could be mitigated by the fact that the cost to produce the ad was zero.

- **Do consider independent and start-up production companies:** This is always my starting point. Independent and start-up production companies do not equal poor quality. They're a small, nimble, and hungry production houses that aren't tied to a specific agency, including social influencers with high-production value and the willingness to simply produce videos (outside content that's specifically aimed at their followers). They will negotiate and work a hundred times harder because they *need* your business, both financially and to enhance their portfolio. There are literally hundreds of options. My experience with this type of studio from Yes Have Some in Atlanta, Georgia, to Clay Cross in Dallas-Fort Worth, Texas, to Galaxy Media in Boston, Massachusetts, to Josh Horton in Los Angeles, California has been nothing short of spectacular. In fact, the extra lift on the front end of finding, performing due diligence, and getting these shops set up with your company is dwarfed by the time savings both during and after production.
- **Make sure the customer is represented:** If tagging a national asset with a retailer logo on an end card isn't the approach you take, make sure to use this opportunity to authentically integrate the customer into your asset. This can manifest itself in multiple ways from being specifically called out in the dialogue ("Let's pick this up at Walmart, where we know the prices are going to be lower"), or the store front could be seen in the background, or a scene can take place in the store. (But please run this by your buyer first and then the store manager. I've never had an issue in the past if done ahead of time).

Does this all work, though? The great news is that video can be measured in a manner very similar to display. Tapping into partners such as RSi, Pathformance, IRi, and so on, can give you store-level, SKU-level data in a test/control environment so you can back into an incremental sales total. This allows you to calculate the GMROI. There are some mediums that are trickier to test, not because of challenges in the methodology but, rather, the lack of vendors that have prioritized the capability due to shopper marketing being ignored or disregarded.

Once you feel that the message type aligns with video and a responsibly priced production solution has been identified, then it's time to make a decision on where the video will be served. If your background is in national media, you're probably thinking that it should be served everywhere. And you're right. But when your budget is $75,000 and not $7,500,00, prioritization is paramount.

Open Web (In-Stream Video)

You are watching CNN and click on a video about an upcoming election, but before the content plays, you are served an ad about organic soup. That would fall in the bucket of an open web in-stream ad. Most of these buys are served programmatically and typically have the lowest costs and most complex targeting capabilities. In fact, the targeting that your partner provides for banner ads or rich media should be exactly the same as video. The wider array of targeting options is a big advantage that open web has over social.

Social (In-Stream, In-Feed Video)

Videos served in social platforms such as YouTube, Facebook/Instagram, and Pinterest should be bucketed as social video. Unlike the open web, there are a handful of unique ad formats that are specific to a platform that can give the brand a few options in trying and delivering its message. The argument for social video is that the audience is more captive. The mindset is different when you are on Facebook versus engaging with sites across the open web. Whether that actually does generate more incremental sales has not been proven, so the responsibility still falls on the shopper marketers to make the best choice for their brand and retailer. The assumed audience mindset will need to overcome two negative aspects of social media: 1) targeting and 2) measurement quirks.

Targeting is primarily limited to the data collected within the social platform itself, so it tends to be interest based with options for geo and demo. If you are going after healthy eaters who shop at Kroger, the targeting would consist of users who "liked" or "followed" Kroger and various healthy food items. This is simply not as accurate and powerful as tapping into Kroger loyalty data or credit card data to prove they are Kroger shoppers. I shop at Kroger on occasion, but I don't follow the store on Facebook or Instagram.

The measurement piece is not as significant because the issues only affect digital metrics and do not apply to YouTube (which is likely to be the most prominent of the social platforms from a video perspective). The most common success metric in video (outside shopper marketing) is video completion rate (VCR). What percentage of those who saw my ad watched the entire video? Seventy-five percent of the video, and so on? Campaigns will then optimize, based on that data: finding similar audience members who are more likely to watch the entire video and, hopefully, more likely to be influenced by the content of the video. For YouTube, in order to be a completed view, the entire video must be viewed. That's good. For Facebook and Instagram, only a fraction of the ad (three seconds, to be exact) has to be viewed to count it as completed. That's not so good. Not only is it an inaccurate representation of the number of folks who actually watched the ad but it derails the optimization. Also, if you are buying on a cost-per-completed-view (CPCV) model, you are paying for a completed views, even when only a small snippet was viewed. Despite this deficiency, incremental sales optimization and attribution should trump VCR. It's a bit difficult to find social video vendor partners that utilize companies such as RSi and IRi for shopper marketing campaigns, but they do exist.

Connected TV (In-Stream)

Chances are that in the course of the last twelve months you've been asked by at least a dozen companies to discuss your connected TV (CTV) strategy. It's every– where—but what is it? Even if you Google-search "connected TV," the answers vary wildly. At the end of the day, it's always best to keep it simple. If you are on a connected device—a smart TV, a gaming console, a mobile phone—and you access any type of over-the-top (OTT) service such as Hulu or Amazon Prime Video or ABC On Demand (typically through an app), the advertising spots available in that experience would fall under the term *connected TV*. Let's say that you missed last night's episode of *The Blacklist* on NBC. You can open up the NBC app on your connected TV or phone or gaming console, scroll over to the shows section, and play the episode on demand. You will be shown ads both before and during the episode. This full episode player inventory would fall under the umbrella of CTV. As you can imagine, when compared to the open web or social media, the inventory is much more limited, hence higher costs. However, audiences are, potentially, the most captive, having made a virtual agreement to sit through ads in order to watch a full episode at their own leisure. You will see video completion rates north of 95% for CTV because who is going to abandon that episode of *The Blacklist* once it's started? Less than 5% of you.

But do high VCR's correlate to incremental sales? Maybe, maybe not. There hasn't been enough widespread testing within shopper marketing to understand that relationship. Are CTV-focused buys worth testing, budget permitting? Definitely. If there is a correlation between completed views and purchases, it's positioned to be a top video medium in the years to come.

At the end of the day, there is a place for video within the world of shopper marketing. However, it's not for every brand and every campaign. Shopper marketers need to weigh budgetary constraints and message type before they decide if video is a tactic to pursue. If so, a sound testing strategy is recommended to understand what inventory sources produce the most effective performance. There has yet to be a clear cut winner due to the lack of detailed testing in the shopper marketing space; the video testing that I've been a part of has shown me that the right message for video and the right targeting can produce extremely positive GMROIs.

Tactic Spotlight: **Interactive Video**

As discussed previously, the merits of video in the shopper marketing space are promising, but within the medium there may even be a tactic that is perfect for shopper marketing and conversion-focused media. Interactive video is not new but the detailed shoppifying of assets

is somewhat of an emerging capability. Tech-savvy firms such as Austin-based KERV Interactive are giving shopper marketers the ability to add multiple click-out points within a video—offering more options for conversions. Once your video asset plays, scenes will auto-populate to an accompanying carousel, and viewers will be directed to click on certain elements via an informative overlay graphic. Each scene can include multiple shoppable elements, and the clickability of the object is down to the pixel level, so no more clunky hot spot polygons. This new form of interactive shoppable video provides multiple opportunities for an engager to be driven to various desired landing spots (such as a product page on or an automatic add-to-cart at a retailer), making it perfect for portfolio buys or brands with multiple pack sizes that address different usage occasions. What this results in is an extremely effective cost per action and a higher average time engaged with the asset. In fact, in my experience, the time engaging with an ad exceeds the length of the ad itself, proving the viability of the interactivity.

The only real drawback, currently, is the lack of access in large inventory platforms such as YouTube and Facebook. If open web inventory is satisfactory, then interactive shoppable video should be in your consideration set. This tactic could end up being the poster child for shopper marketing online video programming.

INFLUENCERS IN SHOPPER MARKETING

I remember it as if it were yesterday: the first time someone tried to explain influencer marketing to me. Granted, they weren't trying to defend the merits of having a Kardashian endorse the product. I got that. It was, at the time time, the relatively new phenomenon of micro-influencers. And they were using it for shopper marketing campaigns! Needless to say, I thought they were joking, but then, that morphed into shock, and then cynicism, and finally, utter disregard for that person as a competent marketer. Now part of my reaction was due to my ignorance of what influencer marketing was and how it was being applied to drive incremental sales in an as efficient a manner as, say, banner ads. But in full transparency, as I dove deeper, I continued to write it off as an all sizzle, no steak product that would prey on shopper marketers who were buying media, based on feel and how good it looked on a slide. It was placed in my slush pile of tactics marked "just because we can, we never asked if we should."

Then, in the blink of an eye, influencer marketing is a major player for marketing/advertising/media dollars.

Shopper marketing and the micro-influencer approach is a growing subindustry with companies such as Collective Bias, Analogy, Linqia, and IZEA grabbing dollars from almost every major CPG organization. And those companies had no issue building up a roster of influencers, because, suddenly, in the United States and across the globe, everyone is influencing via social platforms and blogs. As do many tactics in the digital media world, the influencer space got too big, too soon, especially on the micro-level. I'm not going to spend time on fraudulent audience numbers and misleading engagement because, luckily, much of that has worked itself out over time. That's not to say you shouldn't ask those questions with a prospective vendor partner—you absolutely should—but my focus here is to isolate and amplify influencers role in shopper marketing.

First, to reiterate, when I'm talking influencer market– ing, it's micro-influencers that I'm looking at, not celebrity endorsements. The number of shopper marketing campaigns and executions that can support a top-flight influencer is relatively small; the ones that can afford a bona fide celebrity is even smaller. I worked on two such campaigns in my career. One of the celebrities was living firmly on the B list (Tom Hanks, they were not) and the other was a mid-tier-star athlete (recognizable enough to be in some other national spots but probably not someone your grandma would know). Every other campaign was classic micro-influencer programming.

Influencer Basics

So how does influencer marketing work? In a nutshell, micro-influencers utilize their platforms (it could be a blog, it could be their popular Instagram account, or anything in between) to talk favorably about your brand. This can come in the form of showcasing a recipe in which your brand is the featured ingredient; it could be the perfect kid's birthday party tutorial with your brand front and center in the festivities; it could be a story where your brand was critical in that influencer's life. This content is typically supported with what you hope is striking imagery of your brand. The goal of this user-gener-ated content is to highlight the product or a usage occasion with authenticity, something that is difficult to achieve with typical product shot/logo/stock footage builds from your creative agency. The goal is for it to be persuasive without falling into the same traps as traditional advertising; a subtle push in the right direction versus a more obvious shove.

Where the competitive edges come in is the influencer roster, quality of the content, media amplification strategy (where and how), and measurement. Let's examine these in more detail, as they pertain to shopper marketing.

Roster and Content Quality

Does the roster of influencers matter? Probably not. The dirty little secret is that most influencer marketing firms have access to the same micro-influencers. Since the influencers aren't Kardashians, they usually want/need multiple income sources so why would they ever enter into an exclusive agreement? They wouldn't. So, unless you are trying to get access to a certain celebrity—which we already outlined as being unlikely in the shopper marketing space— the roster is likely similar across potential vendor partners. If you are sending a request for proposal to three different vendors asking for influencers that resonate with Walmart shoppers from the southern United States and can highlight quick and easy recipes, there could be some overlap on the recommendation.

Conversely, the quality of the content *does* matter. Whether you subscribe to my theory that it's less about the organic reach/impact of the influencer and more of a creative strategy, *or* you believe that influencers are effective in driving incremental sales, you need good content. You need authentic and moving content. Despite there being a massive overlap in available influencers, the standards with which those influencers are held on an individual project does vary. Influencer company A might have certain restrictions around the type of photography, and company B might be a bit more lax. Sure, a cell phone selfie is fine! Two quick bits of advice here: 1) be upfront, in writing, with the vendor partner, about the quality you expect, and 2) always check the past work of any influencer being considered for your campaign (even though vendors check for competitive posts/recommendations and blatant no-no's such as hate speech or cursing, they don't always audit the more subjective quality of the imagery).

If you take away anything from this section, let it be this: **micro-influencer content for shopper marketing campaigns need to highlight the retailer**. Just tagging the retailer in the copy is not good enough. The rule of thumb that I like to use is that any image that is being used for amplification (more on that in the next paragraph), when viewed out of context, must be recognizable as a shopper marketing ad. If it's not, then it's not a shopper marketing program. For example, that beautifully shot image of the cutting board with perfectly sliced vegetables all dancing around a bottle of your brand's secret, scrumptious, can't-miss sauce better have a Walmart bag next to it so anyone engaging with that content knows that it's about getting that secret, scrumptious, can't-miss sauce *at Walmart*. If the influencer wants to take a photo of them, all dressed up like every other urban millennial stock photo actor, imbibing a cool refreshing bottle of your ultrahealthy, organic, fair-trade kombucha, the background better have a clear shot of Kroger so those who are engaging with it know it's about your brand *at Kroger*.

Amplification Strategies

The content is crucial, yes, but more importantly, it's how they plan on amplifying the media. In a perfect world, you can gain access to the influencers and manage the amplification in-house. Unfortunately, that's not the standard practice currently. The influencer marketers make their margins on up-charging for media, not on influencer access fees. And as much as your influencer vendor friends don't want to admit it, the paid media piece is what's driving performance, not the organic reach of these micro-influencers. Influencers on the scale of—you guessed it—a Kardashian have a reach that is meaningful. Influencers of five to a hundred thousand followers probably are making very little impact from their organic posts, at least not enough for a campaign to pay for itself. But the millions of ad impressions using their imagery *can*—at least, in theory. I would focus your efforts, when comparing potential vendors, on their media prowess and recommended strategy. First and foremost, what's the mix of paid media versus influencer fees? Some companies will say that 70% of the costs are going to contract the influencers and their content, leaving 30% to amplify. That, right there, says this company believes that the owned reach of these influencers is going to drive lower funnel conversion for your brand at a given retailer. And they would be wrong. Avoid these like the plague. If it's the opposite (or close to it), then you might have a chance for the campaign to perform against an ROI/GMROI KPI. However, you are still left with this simple question: Is the authentic and better user-generated creative (plus any bumps from the influencers' owned reach) going to outperform our standard creative by three to six times (assuming that standard creative might make up 5 to 10% of your budget, if that)? If you think I'm crazy for even saying that, then remove influencer marketing from your consideration set immediately. If you believe it could happen, then you can start testing to see if this is the case.

Second, most of the influencer marketing companies such as Facebook, Instagram, Pinterest, and Twitter stay within the well-established platforms to amplify content. There is nothing wrong with any of these. However, note that your targeting is limited to whatever data exists within these platforms. For example, Facebook is going to be more intent- and interest-based; you won't have the luxury of purchase-based targeting. You know they "like" your brand or "like" your key retailer, but you don't know if they actually buy your product or shop at that store. This is more of an issue across all influencer marketing companies, and those that also offer open web extension might provide a better targeting approach.

· · ·

Measuring Influencer Campaigns

Measurement has been something that influencer marketing companies have strategically avoided for some time, and it was the cause of my first eye roll when I was initially approached about the space. The usual suspects of engagements, clicks, and views were considered acceptable. If you were lucky, you might also be provided a report on the time spent onsite to further validate the content that featured your product. None of this tells you the full story, principally the final chapter: did it drive sales? By the time you are reading this, the list of companies offering this service may have quadrupled (which would be a good thing), but I've found one particular influencer company that is dedicated to giving shopper marketers a meaningful, business-oriented metric. That company is Inmar-owned Collective Bias, which as partnered with Ansa, a tried-and-true product offering from RSi, to provide an incremental sales lift with, on most occasions, statistical significance. Whether this is a smart move by Collective Bias for their business remains to be seen (early signs were quite positive), but for the first time, you can back into a legitimate GMROI on an influencer campaign. The time of relying on anecdotal proof and playing to the emotional connection of shopper marketers is over for micro-influencer buys. They now have to actually work. And that's a good thing for shopper marketers.

Influencer campaigns are no longer in my slush pile as I was wrong to dismiss them from the word go. However, just because they are out of my slush pile doesn't mean they don't need to prove their effectiveness for shopper marketing, or they will wind up in my trash can.

CONSIDERING IN-STREAM AUDIO

Much like digital video, in-stream audio hasn't widely been thought of as a shopper marketing tool. You're saying that a thirty-second Pandora audio spot drives sales of my brand at my focus retailer? You're telling me a Spotify listener is going to be influenced by an advertisement between songs to buy my brand at my key retailer? These are fair questions and ones that should have been asked. But the answer is, well, yes. Yes, they can.

In-stream audio is a relatively broad term because the entire ad experience can also include visual elements such as companion banners, but the heart of the tactic is a fifteen- or thirty-second ad read during a potential shopper's listening experience on platforms such as Pandora, Spotify, Apple Podcasts, TuneIn, and iHeartRadio. Most of what we are going to talk about today is music focused but as podcasts continue to rise, more inventory will be opened up in that space. Each platform has its own subtle nuances within its offering, but they are all fairly similar.

As I was planning programming across multiple brands for 2019 executions, in-stream audio was an afterthought, not even a small curiosity. However, when a particular program popped up that was built around utilizing our product to enhance a shopper's party or social get together, audio snuck into the consideration set. We could do a fun and festive ad read and see if that connected to Walmart shoppers while they were listening to fun and festive music. The best part about this buy was that the company we chose, Pandora, had a relationship with RSi, so we could measure incremental sales impact of the buy. I knew this would be a one-and-done with audio. And I was dead wrong. The program performed admirably, not a top performer for the year, but the best tactic on this particular buy. But you should never build a plan around the results of a single test. So, I tested again on a few programs that would align with audio as a tactic. One was a spooky, Halloween-themed read; the other was silly and irreverent. I also decided to not rely on a single inventory source such as Pandora and work with companies that could tap into multiple sources and still use RSi to measure sales impact. Goodway Group was my choice. And both programs performed extremely well. In fact, these were two of the top five performers for the year for our business at Walmart. I continued to test, and more often than not, audio worked. The few times it did not were when I tried to force the tactic into a campaign message because I was enamored with the recent positive results. At the end of the day, 75% of our in-stream audio executions exceeded internal GMROI benchmarks and, for the year, audio's average GMROI was over $1.50. Our average program cost was a very shopper marketing friendly $50,000.

As we dove deeper, the multiplatform approach proved stronger than the single platform, which makes sense, especially since many of the multiplatform aggregators include all of the major players (Pandora, Spotify, iHeart, etc.). It also affords the ability to include RSi for Spotify and iHeart Radio buys since they don't include that in their solo offering. In fact, I'm not sure Spotify and iHeart know what shopper marketing even means.

At the end of the day, in-stream audio could be a viable shopper marketing tool to increase sales of your brand at your retailer. However, the key is to not force audio into a campaign that doesn't lend itself to the medium. If it's a new flavor of a soda or a new count of toilet paper rolls, audio probably isn't necessary. But if you want to convey some emotion and need a few seconds to explain a benefit (without the need of video), audio should be considered, especially if it's for a retailer with RSi access. Lastly, start with a multiplatform approach since you aren't putting your eggs in a single platform basket, and it opens up sales lift testing on inventory sources that don't offer it directly.

COOKING UP SALES WITH RECIPE NETWORKS

Over the last few years, the emergence of recipe networks into the digital media landscape has been fascinating. Shopper marketing has been impacted by this tactic's rise to prominence as well, but is it right for your brand and retailer? It's a tough question, but one you can easily answer with some thoughtful planning and sound vendor and measurement choices.

First and foremost, is the environment of a recipe network right for your brand? We will discuss this in a bit, but that doesn't mean your product can be used *in a recipe*; plenty of nonrecipe items successfully tap into the media power of a recipe network. If you're dealing with toilet paper, you're probably not going to consider a recipe network (inset bad chili joke here as the exception), but if you're a paper plate brand, then being associated with barbecue recipes or party appetizers might not be the worst thing in the world. But assuming your brand is directly or indirectly relevant, let's discuss the two types of networks and the two prominent types of ad formats.

Let's discuss Allrecipes (by Meredith) versus Chicory.

By no means are these the only two options, but I think they best represent the two types of recipe networks. Allrecipes is a power-house with widespread appeal and name recognition. It's a publisher-direct model in which you're putting your hopes and dreams in the hands of a single entity. But they have very large hands. They are "it" when it comes to go-to recipe inspiration. They have the monthly uniques to prove it too. Chicory, on the other hand, is a network of recipe sites and blogs that join forces to create a formidable foe to Allrecipes. With Chicory, you lose instant name recognition, but you get diversity and scale without paying premium rates. It's publisher-direct versus ad-network philosophy. Both have their merits and their challenges. You might not know, right off the bat, which approach is better for your brand and retailer, but you can determine if recipe networks are even worth exploring.

All potential vendors in this space have their own unique capabil-ities and twists on the tactic, but I want to focus on the two ad types that are ubiquitous in the recipe network space: the pairing ad and the branded ingredient. The good news is that they are both as they sound. The pairing ad is a display ad that rides along with a certain recipe. This would be where the paper plate product mentioned above could play. A shopper sees a recipe for pork sliders, perfect for a backyard barbecue and, right below the last ingredient, is a nice ad reminding them to stock up on paper plates at Target. Even more self-explanatory is the branded ingredient. This would be where your product is featured as one of the ingredients. In that pork slider recipe, instead of saying "slider buns," it would actually say brand X slider buns, and when you add the items to your cart from the recipe, brand X's slider buns would be included. On that topic, most recipe network offerings have some sort of add-to-cart/list functionality, though some are more advanced than others. This is critical because it gives the shoppers the ability to add all of the items to their cart to make the recipe. So, don't you want your item as part of that?

Okay, recipe networks are pretty enticing. I get that. But do they work? Do they actually drive incremental sales in an efficient manner. In my experience, the answer is: sometimes. In a previous study that I was part of, the more premium publisher-direct model would drive incremental sales but not enough to offset costs. It was not a 1:1 gross margin return. A few caveats to these tests: 1) there were not enough done to definitively say that they could *never* produce a good GMROI; 2) the products being tested had extremely low margins, so anything over 40% would have paid out; and 3) the tests were all done at a single retailer (so I can't say if the poor performance had to do with the specific retailer and it could have worked at another retailer). I think a higher margin brand that has natural synergies in the recipe world would be worth testing. On the ad network-style buys, the ability to conduct incremental sales lift testing through companies such as RSi is relatively new. My gut feeling is that they will also struggle to produce positive ROIs, but their flexibility and lower CPMs lead me to believe that they will, ultimately, win the recipe network war on the shopper marketing front.

But are recipes networks a shopper marketing tool? Yes, absolutely. But tread lightly.

SHOPPER MARKETING & DIGITAL MEDIA QUICK HITS

As you go through life as a shopper marketer, here are some additional quick hitters to be aware of. Most are common-sense observations, but that won't stop vendors from trying to sneak them in and influence decisions.

Digital metrics do not correlate with sales. Higher click-through rates do not equal sales. Higher incremental store visits do not equal sales.

Targeting efficiency helps produce the best GMROIs. Don't determine that you need to serve media around X number of stores; choose to serve media around X number of dollars represented. If 20% of a retailer's stores make up 50% of your sales, make sure to include those stores. Focus and improve your targeting efficiency. Fish where the fish are.

. . .

**Data is the not most important aspect of digital ...
every time.** See the entire Six Pillars approach. Data might be the
most important aspect if it ladders up to the objective in a more
convincing way than tech, media, attribution, and so on. Also, great
data that is optimized on poor technology or can't be measured with
proper attribution or is so expensive it destroys your ROI is not really
great.

Return-on-Ad Spend ("ROAS") **does not measure incrementality**. This is a big one. Most vendors report on ad-attributed
or media- attributed sales, meaning that every sale from someone
exposed to your ad gets counted toward the ROAS. We don't know if
that sale would have happened anyway. So, please make sure you are
seeing *incremental* ROAS (iROAS)

**Viewability, in most cases, should not guide digital
media decisions in shopper marketing**. It's true that an ad
which isn't seen can't influence sales. No argument there. And if ads
that are more likely to be seen cost the same as those that have more
risk of not being seen cost the exact same, then you could ignore this
bullet point altogether. Let's say you have $1. For that $1, I can get
you four ads, each with a 90% chance of being seen. Three of the four
end up being seen—a respectable viewability of 75%. For that same
$1, I can get you 20 ads with a 40% chance of being seen—and seven
of the 20 are actually seen—a not-so stellar 35% viewability. But your
raw number of views is higher, seven to three, and you now have
seven opportunities to influence sales, rather than three. Net net,
optimizing on viewability should be left to national media folks and
their endless budgets and fluff success metrics.

Tagging a national media program with a retailer logo

is not shopper marketing. This could be an entire book. The presence of a logo does not make it a shopper marketing campaign. If that national media program has a logo, is targeted to the specific retailer shopper profile, is being optimized and measured on sales at that single account, and ladders up to the object at that single retailer, then yes, it's a shopper campaign. In my experience, national media programming will simply include a logo and maybe some geo and call it shopper marketing. This thinking needs to be eliminated from CPG organizations.

You don't need 85% statistical significance to gain insights. Yes, it helps and keeps data scientists off your back, especially on sales KPIs. However, if you only get directional data, that's better than no data. And building test designs around previous learnings from directional data is a better approach than pulling hypotheses out of thin air to test. We should all strive for significance, but it shouldn't be an all-or-nothing mindset.

You need to have realistic success benchmarks for innovation. New products should never follow the same success target as your base business. You might need a $1.25 GMROI on your base brand, but maybe your new item should only require a $0.50 GMROI since you're going to have to spend a little more to generate trial. If you can model out the lifetime value of a new consumer, even better.

1+1 = 3 is a real thing ... sometimes. If your national media program and shopper marketing program work together, it could be more successful than the two working independently. But it's no guarantee. It could be as simple as once shoppers are exposed to five national ads or engaged with a national ad and meet the criteria for your retailer (geo, etc.), you serve them a shopper ad with a strong call-to-action. The test designs on these are trickier but can be done. In addition, in-store marketing and digital marketing together can produce a better GMROI than if the two marketing approaches are executed in isolation. Sometimes. The takeaway here is don't assume a simply overlay is going to produce exponentially better results. Make sure the execution is thoughtfully designed, optimized, and measured. Continue to iterate until you get that 1+1=3.

Don't always default to animated banners over static banners even though they are the same cost. If your message is super simple, get to the point with a static banner. Even light animation can be zoomed over without seeing the benefit callout or CTA. Even in this day and age, there are people that have connectivity issues where the load time on a basic HTML5 ad could prevent them from seeing the main message of that ad.

THE SIX PILLARS
APPROACH EXERCISES

EXERCISES

These exercises are entirely hypothetical but meant to show how the Six Pillars Approach can get you from "Eeeeek, what do I do now?" to a strategically sound digital media plan.

Now, let's see the Six Pillars Approach in action.

CASE #1

THE BRIEF

You are the shopper marketer on a soda brand supporting Walmart. You are introducing a new flavor, strawberry, because of a shopper insight that Walmart carbonated-soft-drink shoppers are over-indexing on flavored soda purchases. Your current portfolio has a cola, orange, and grape flavor. The new strawberry extension is not being supported by national media as it is not deemed a tier-1 priority. The main reason for the new flavor is to reenergize sluggish sales of the entire soda line at a few key accounts such as Walmart. Leadership wants to know if new flavors can really lift the entire portfolio, because they are also considering a lemon-line extension later in the year. Unfortunately, your company has not been testing your digital media executions, so there isn't anything from a past performance standpoint to help guide your decision. Your budget is $50,000.

ESTABLISHING THE ROOF

. . .

Step 1A: Define your primary KPI.

At the end of the day, it seems that the goal is to increase sales at Walmart for the entire line of soda, with the new strawberry flavor being the catalyst for generating excitement and, ultimately, driving the sale. Your KPI should be total incremental sales—and you'll need to show these in a definitive manner since leadership is asking for a report card on this buy to know if it can be replicated down the road.

Step 1B: Is the message simple or complex? What will it take to communicate the message effectively?

Communicating a flavor such as strawberry should be considered quite simple, as most shoppers will know the flavor profile of a strawberry. If your flavor extension were something like Rockin' Rad Explosion, it might require more explanation, but strawberry is pretty straightforward. Based on the message, spending money on producing custom video doesn't seem necessary unless you already have national assets available (which you don't since it's not being supported nationally). Digital video is out. Other long-form digital such as audio and influencers could be thrown out here since there isn't a need to spend the premiums to explain strawberry flavoring.

One additional element to note is that the goal is to lift the entire portfolio, so the creative should champion the strawberry but also include the other flavors to remind the shopper that there are multiple options. If the cola, orange, and grape aren't shown, you are missing out on potential halo lift across the line.

Now that you've landed on a KPI and understand what's necessary to communicate your message, you can employ the Six Pillars Approach.

RANKING THE SIX PILLARS

· · ·

Before you start, you can rule out **PAST PERFORMANCE** as the first pillar because the previous shopper marketer did not measure the campaigns or failed to keep track of the results.

You can also rule out video, audio, and influencers as potential tactics since a long-form communication is not recommended for a simple flavor extension.

Based on your KPI, you need to drive incremental sales of the soda line—and show if the program was successful. If you can't show the results, then the program was a failure internally. Your first pillar is **ATTRIBUTION**. Since you are supporting Walmart, that leaves open any vendor with access to Ansa by RSi or programming via Walmart Media Group (retailer media network).

From a tactical standpoint, you can measure incremental sales on display, recipe networks (pairing ads, specifically), and retailer media networks. The only new tactic to be discarded should be onsite search.

But wait! Don't forget about your budget. The Attribution pillar is not simply if they *can* measure but what are the minimums to unlock the measurement? Walmart Media Group has a minimum well above your $50,000 budget. So, retailer media networks should be thrown into the tactic trash bin.

So, after attribution, what is the next most important pillar? Your shopper insights were focused on Walmart CSD shoppers, so making sure you are serving ads to the right shopper will likely be important. Because **DATA** will determine the ability to confidently target those shoppers, it's the second pillar.

You know that you can tap into great data to determine Walmart shoppers and CSD shoppers with display. Can you do that with recipe networks? Yes, to some degree, but it's more about purchase intent than actual known shoppers. With display, you can layer in deterministic credit card purchase data to confirm Walmart shoppers. With recipe networks, it may be that they clicked on a previous

Walmart ad within their network or they live near a Walmart (don't we all?). Since there is a big discrepancy in the ability to target Walmart shoppers and CSD shoppers, display should be prioritized over recipe network pairing ads.

After only two pillars, you've already landed on the right tactic for the buy. **Digital display**. That's the magic of the Six Pillars Approach.

As we keep going, we can help identify the right vendor partner.

What we already know: the partner must be able to measure incremental sales at or below a $50,000 investment and target Walmart shoppers and CSD shoppers.

At this point, you might have it narrowed down to three vendor partners that you are familiar with that fit this profile. How can we narrow it even further? What pillar is the next most important to achieving your KPI of incremental sales at Walmart?

Could it be technology? You definitely want a platform that can optimize optimally.

Could it be media? Maybe the contextual relevance of the inventory could drive performance.

Could it be pricing? The lower the rates, the better the chance of producing better GMROI.

The case can be made for all three. You get to choose, and there isn't a wrong answer—that is, until you test them all over time. Once you decide what you feel is the most critical, you can continue to trim the vendor partner field.

For this example, I am going to rank **TECHNOLOGY** as the most important. One of the vendors utilizes multiple demand-side platforms (DSP) to optimize across, so you are getting optimizations within each DSP and across the entire roster. The other two vendors use their own DSP. Both are AI-driven with manual oversight, but one of them does not have a cross-device graph.

Immediately, I can eliminate the one without a cross- device graph.

I now have a multi-DSP option and a single DSP option; both are sound from a technology standpoint, so I really want to go one more pillar down.

To me, the next most important pillar in producing a solid GMROI is **PRICING**. The multi-DSP vendor is intriguing because I think the additional inter-DSP optimizations could improve performance, however, the CPM for this vendor is $5.25. The single DSP vendor is $3.75. Both have a $0.75 CPM up-charge to partner with RSi for the attribution.

Now, I only have to answer one question: Do I feel that the benefits of having multiple DSPs to optimize across warrant a $1.50/M premium? I do not.

I choose the solo DSP partner with the $3.75/M rate, plus the $0.75/M RSi upcharge to execute my digital display ad highlighting my soda portfolio with the new strawberry SKU as the hero.

This is the Six Pillars Approach in action. Instead of choosing between multiple digital tactics and an endless roster of vendor partners, the objective-focused pillar strategy narrowed it down to where you were able to identify the best tactic to achieve your objective on the second pillar; and select a vendor partner based on your instinctual ranking of the top four pillars.

To recap this example:

. . .

KPI/Message:

   Tactics: Ruled out video, audio, influencers.

   Partners: Ruled out all video, audio, and influencer partners.

1. ATTRIBUTION

   Tactics: Ruled out retailer media networks and onsite search.

   Partners: Ruled out Walmart Media Group and any digital display partners that can't measure incremental sales.

2. DATA

   Tactics: Ruled out recipe network pairing ads.

   (DIGITAL DISPLAY IS YOUR CHOICE.)

   Partners: Ruled out recipe network partners and any digital display partners that can't target Walmart and CSD shoppers confidently.

3. TECHNOLOGY

   Tactics: Digital display recommended.

   Partners: Ruled out partner C for not having a cross-device graph.

4. PRICING

   Tactics: Digital display recommended.

   Partners: Ruled partner A because the $1.50/M premium didn't justify the better optimization opportunity of the multiple DSPs. **(PARTNER B IS YOUR CHOICE.)**

   5. MEDIA: Did not factor in.

   6. PAST PERFORMANCE: No past campaign data exists.

   Now let's look at a few more examples.

CASE #2

THE BRIEF

You are the shopper marketer on a premium frozen fish brand supporting Target. You want to highlight your efforts in sustainability because of a shopper insight that Target shoppers will pay more for their grocery items if they feel the brand is socially and/or environmentally conscious. You also know from consumer research that people, regardless of where they shop, don't associate frozen food companies with being leaders in environmental causes. At the end of the day, you need to drive incremental sales, primarily from fresh seafood buyers, competitive frozen fish brands, or other Target shoppers who may be influenced by your brand's sustainability efforts. Your volume is very low at Target. It is acceptable to target at the category-level and potentially serve ads to existing buyers (even though frequency isn't the primary objective, due to the small base). Your benchmark for success is a GMROI of $0.80. You are fine with a short-term GMROI that does not pay back because of a history of excellent repeat purchases. Unfortunately, your company has not been testing your digital media executions, so there isn't anything from a past performance standpoint to help guide your decision. Your budget is $75,000.

ESTABLISHING THE ROOF

Step 1A: Define your primary KPI.

Drive incremental sales, primarily but not exclusively, through household penetration. The success metric is GMROI and the benchmark is $0.80.

Step 1B: Is the message simple or complex? What will it take to communicate the message effectively?

Sustainability is not only a complex message but carries with it the potential for an emotional and personal connection. The average shopper at Target might not know what sustainability really entails and therefore needs education and convincing.

Due to this, a simple digital display ad is not going to suffice on communicating this message. Yes, you can get more banner ads in the market than you can longer-form content, but if it can't be digested by shoppers in a few seconds, you might as well have not served the ad at all.

So, you can already eliminate a few tactics. Digital display (even rich media) would have a hard time communicating the message to the Target shoppers. Recipe networks and onsite search would also not be able to achieve success in this area. Audio is typically a viable option here, but you feel that visuals are necessary to evoke an emotional response with the shopper. Audio is out. This leaves video, influencers, and the long-form elements of Roundel, Target's retailer media networks (primarily, onsite video) in the consideration set.

The roof has been built. Now on to the pillars!

. . .

RANKING THE SIX PILLARS

Before you start, you can rule out **PAST PERFORMANCE** as you are, once again, left without any past data.

You've ruled out all tactics but video, influencers, and some offerings within the retailer media network Roundel. Based on your KPI, you need to produce a GMROI of $0.80. In order to back into a significant GMROI, you need to understand the raw incremental sales generated by the campaign.

Thus, **ATTRIBUTION** is the first pillar. Since you are supporting Target, that leaves open any vendor with access to Ansa by RSi or programming via Roundel.

From a tactical standpoint, video and influencers both can be measured via RSi. So they can both stay. However, Roundel requires a larger investment to get an incremental sales total. It is are out.

Next, since not only your brand but the frozen fish category has a relatively low household penetration, you want to make sure you are —dare I say it—fishing where the fish are.

Forgive me, please. **DATA** is pillar #2. Though influencers are pretty solid at finding Target shoppers, they fail to video on two fronts: 1) they can find Target shoppers (location and interest targeting) but not as confidently as your video vendors (location, interest, Target app downloads, and credit card usage), and 2) they aren't as strong on understanding shoppers who buy the frozen meat categories (regardless of the retailer).

Once again, you have landed on the recommended tactic after only two pillars: **digital video**. But, even more, you've ruled out social video since you would be relegated to the same targeting issues as influencers: interest and location.

Now, on to the vendor selection. We've already determined that the vendor must be able to give us incremental Target sales with a

$75,000 budget and be able to isolate Target shoppers buying the frozen fish/meat or fresh fish/meat categories.

But what next? Technology, media, or pricing?

You feel that the entire video needs to be consumed to really influence shoppers into buying the product at Target. Therefore, a CPCV pricing model is ideal.

PRICING becomes the next pillar. This leaves two potential digital vendor partners you are aware of: partner A and partner B; both of their CPCV rates are nearly identical.

Since you offer numerous frozen fish options—barramundi, cod, salmon, and snapper—you feel that a partner with the technology to link out to product pages at various scenes within the video spot would improve conversion and performance.

You place **TECHNOLOGY** as the next pillar. Only partner A can leverage this new interactive technology, so partner A is your choice.

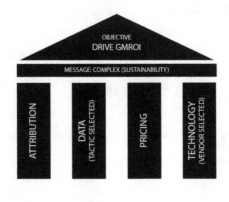

To recap this example:

KPI/Message:

Tactics: Ruled out digital display, audio, recipe network, onsite search, and many elements of retailer media networks.

Partners: Ruled out digital display, audio, recipe network, and onsite search partners.

1. ATTRIBUTION

Tactics: Ruled out retailer media networks.

Partners: Ruled out Roundel and any video and influencers partners that can't measure incremental sales.

2. DATA

Tactics: Ruled out influencers. **(OPEN WEB IN- STREAM VIDEO IS YOUR CHOICE.)**

Partners: Ruled out influencer partners and video partners that focus on social video.

3. PRICING

Tactics: Video recommended.

Partners: Ruled out any video partner that can't do CPCV pricing.

4. TECHNOLOGY

Tactics: Video recommended.

Partners: Ruled out partner B for not offering interactive overlays to make all of your featured items in the video shoppable. **(PARTNER A IS YOUR CHOICE.)**

5. MEDIA: Did not factor in.

6. PAST PERFORMANCE: No past campaign data exists.

THE BRIEF

You are the shopper marketer for a toothpaste brand supporting Walgreens. The company is launching a new organic toothpaste because of a consumer insight that more and more households are shifting their nonfood item purchases to organic and all-natural varieties, and toothpaste is an emerging category in that space. Your shopper insight is that typical Walgreens shoppers will make a special trip specifically for toothpaste, so getting on their list in a timely manner is essential. The national team is planning an all-out, 360-degree marketing campaign starting in July, but the product starts rolling out at Walgreens in May. The rollout will likely be sporadic. However, the national team is hoping for some early success at Walgreens. In addition, your buyers aren't 100% sold on this new organic toothpaste and has hinted that they won't wait for it to hit its stride. Your objective is to start selling as much product as possible as soon as the first store gets it on shelf—and you need to do so in the most efficient manner. Unfortunately, your company has not been testing your digital media executions, so there isn't anything from a past performance standpoint to help guide your decision. Your budget is $40,000.

ESTABLISHING THE ROOF

Step 1A: Define your primary KPI.

Drive velocity of the new product at Walgreens without wasting money.

Step 1B: Is the message simple or complex? What will it take to communicate the message effectively?

Shoppers might not understand the subtle nuances of how an item gets to be labeled "organic," but they under– stand that "organic" products are "better," and they accept the premium price point.

Right out of the gate, this unique KPI can really only be achieved via Ansa by RSi's first scan programming (see "First Scan Optimization" chapter). The good news is that almost every digital tactic is represented by a handful of vendors that have partnerships with RSi.

The message is simple, so digital display will remain a considered tactic. Video, audio, and recipe networks don't really fit. Walgreens does not have an acceptable retailer media network in the same vein as Walmart and Kroger, among others. Influencers, though not simple, could be considered because the individual creators could provide credible social proof on how good the new toothpaste is—and the social amplification could tap into the RSi first scan.

The roof has been built. Now on to the pillars!

RANKING THE SIX PILLARS

. . .

Before you start, you can rule out **PAST PERFORMANCE** as you are, once again, left without any past data.

You've ruled out all tactics but display and influencers, both using RSi first scan data to eliminate waste.

You aren't being asked to showcase any statistically significant results—simply to serve ads around stores as soon as you know they have the product on shelf. Attribution isn't critical here, just the relationship with RSi to use the first scan data. After that, you want to make sure you are serving ads to Walgreens shoppers who do place some importance on organic products.

DATA should be next. I know you don't need to use data to find toothpaste buyers, since the household penetration is close to 100%—and organic toothpaste buyers would be such a small audience to target. But that doesn't mean data isn't critical. You might not need to know if they are likely to buy toothpaste (since everyone should be in this set), but it's a lot to ask any digital media execution to convince someone who has never cared about items being organic or all-natural to suddenly start caring *and* start with toothpaste. So, identifying organic shoppers who also shop at Walgreens is paramount.

Based on your shopper insight, you also know toothpaste is a planned trip to Walgreens, which is rare for small-format stores (drug stores, convenience stores, etc.). Understanding where shoppers are in the purchase cycle of something such as toothpaste is extremely important. If you serve them an ad a week after they made a purchase at Walgreens or another retailer, that's a wasted impression. This is tricky data to get, but some *vendor* partners can get there. *Influencer* partners can't.

Digital display is your choice—and after only one pillar!

You are aware of two partners that execute digital display, can confidently target Walgreens shoppers and shoppers who value organic items and can, to some degree, factor in purchase cycle. Neither one stands above the other in this pillar.

To help us select a vendor, we go to the next pillar. Attribution? No, we've covered that you aren't expected to do anything other than drive velocity and not waste the dollars. Technology? There doesn't seem to be a specific need regarding optimization capabilities. Media? The ad formats and inventory aren't that critical (beyond the obvious table stakes regarding fraud and nonhuman traffic). Everything seems to be equal.

So, which one is cheaper? Which one gives you more bang for your buck, be it a lower rate or some meaningful added value.

PRICING is the next pillar. And the last one. Partner A is 10% cheaper than partner B for essentially the same offering. So, partner A it is!

To recap this example:

KPI/Message:

Tactics: Ruled out video, audio, and recipe networks (note: retailer media networks and onsite search not an option for this retailer).

Partners: Ruled out video, audio, and recipe network partners; any digital display or influencer partner that can't tap into the RSi first scan data.

1. DATA

Tactics: Ruled out influencers. **(DIGITAL DISPLAY IS YOUR CHOICE.)**

Partners: Ruled out influencer partners.

2. PRICING

Tactics: Digital display recommended.

Partners: Ruled out partner B. **(PARTNER A IS YOUR CHOICE.)**

3. TECHNOLOGY: Did not factor in.

4. MEDIA: Did not factor in.

5. ATTRIBUTION: Did not factor in.

6. PAST PERFORMANCE: No past campaign data exists.

CASE #4

THE BRIEF

You are the shopper marketer for a baking morsel brand supporting Walmart. The company has seen some soft sales recently and can't afford to have that continue during the key holiday season. Your shopper insight is that typical Walmart shoppers are looking more at recipe hacks that are convenient, quick, and tasty. They are not as concerned about health benefits. Your objective is to make sure that your brand is on the list as the morsel of choice when the shoppers are searching and planning their holiday recipes. You, personally, want to show that your digital execution was successful as there has been a lot of talk from senior leadership that digital doesn't work in your category. Unfortunately, your company has not been testing your digital media executions, so there isn't anything from a past performance standpoint to help guide your decision. Your budget is $50,000.

. . .

ESTABLISHING THE ROOF

Step 1A: Define your primary KPI.

Get your morsels on shoppers' list as they plan their holiday recipes. You have a secondary, personal KPI of showcasing that this approach can be successful at generating a strong GMROI.

Step 1B: Is the message simple or complex? What will it take to communicate the message effectively?

The message is easy to understand ("Choose us as your ingredient"), but since it needs to be recipe focused, certain tactics will have to be ruled out.

Both the KPI and message scream "recipe"—and communicating your brand's role in holiday recipes will be paramount. Because of this, we must reduce the consideration set to the best vehicles for recipe influence: recipe networks (obviously), influencers, and video. Audio, digital display, retailer media networks, and onsite search are not viable for this type of program.

Your personal KPI should be treated as *nice* to have, not *need* to have. You don't want to sacrifice getting the best choice of a program just for the opportunity to prove success with statistically significant results. Chances are, if you pick your program to accommodate that opportunity, the risk of poor performance is higher. Let's hope that you can have your cake and eat it too.

The roof has been built. Now on to the pillars!

RANKING THE SIX PILLARS

Before you start, you can rule out **PAST PERFORMANCE** as you are, once again, left without any past data.

You've ruled out all tactics but recipe networks, influencers, and video. Now what?

You are being tasked with getting your ingredient on lists and in carts of shoppers as they build their holiday recipe plans. You need to be *with* or *in* recipes. The contextual relevance of the ad is going to drive performance against your stated objective.

So, **MEDIA** should be priority number one.

Not only do you want to be in an environment where recipes are highlighted but you want to make sure they are focused on convenience and ease-of-prep, per your shopper insight.

Recipe networks can definitely accommodate these needs. As can influencers. Video assets can showcase recipes but the costs to have them only served on recipe sites would be astronomical; and a more cost-effective open web approach loses the contextual relevance, so video is out.

You are now down to two tactics: recipe networks and influencers.

You feel that both recipe networks and influencers could work for this buy, so you want to pulse in your secondary KPI of showcasing performance on sales. To you, this supersedes data (because both tactics have vendors that have the same strengths and limitations in targeting).

ATTRIBUTION would be next. This makes it an easy choice because you aren't aware of any influencer vendor that can optimize on incremental sales for $50,000. Your choice is a **recipe network** buy. Their minimums are $90,000. In fact, you only know of one recipe network partner (partner A) that can do this, so that partner is your choice.

Data, technology, and pricing did not even factor into the selection.

To recap this example:

KPI/Message:

Tactics: Ruled out digital display, audio, onsite search, and retailer media networks.

Partners: Ruled out digital display, audio, onsite search, and retailer media networks.

1. MEDIA

Tactics: Ruled out video.

Partners: Ruled out video partners.

2. ATTRIBUTION

Tactics: Ruled out influencers. **(RECIPE NETWORK IS YOUR CHOICE.)**

Partners: Ruled out recipe network partners that can't measure for $50K. **(PARTNER A IS YOUR CHOICE.)**

3. DATA: Did not factor in.

4. TECHNOLOGY: Did not factor in.

5. PRICING: Did not factor in.

6. PAST PERFORMANCE: No past campaign data exists.

CASE #5

THE BRIEF

You are the shopper marketer for a condiment brand supporting Meijer. The category has high household penetration but a strong private label presence. Your shopper insight is that typical Meijer shoppers don't have any significant loyalty to any brand in your category. They just buy whatever is cheapest. Based on this fact, your trade team will be funding a retailer-specific promotion during the summer to align with grilling/barbecue season. Your objective is to drive as many incremental purchases as possible of your brand at Meijer during the summer months. In the past, your team has executed two digital media executions at Meijer, both using Ansa by RSi, to measure incremental sales. A rich media (interactive mobile interstitial ads) program supporting a similar summer campaign during the previous year yielded a respectable $1.05 GMROI, and an in-stream audio program supporting last year's tailgating campaign, generated a strong $1.65 GMROI. Due to some cuts, your budget for this program is only $28,000.

. . .

ESTABLISHING THE ROOF

Step 1A: Define your primary KPI.

Drive incremental sales. Produce a strong GMROI.

Step 1B: Is the message simple or complex? What will it take to communicate the message effectively?

It's an extremely simple message since the household penetration of the category is high. The creative will be summer themed, highlighting backyard barbecues and grilling. All forms of digital media can accommodate this visual.

However, even though the message is very simple, it could be conveyed in a variety of manners, from a simple image of the product in the appropriate setting to influencers discussing their favorite grilling recipes made better by your brand.

But wait! You are also running a promotion during this time. This needs to be accounted for in the message. The promotion itself isn't overly complicated ("Buy our brand and get 50% off a private label hot dog or hamburger bun"), but it makes it a bit more difficult to communicate via a static or light animation digital display ad.

Based on the KPI and message requirements, you've ruled out digital display (less rich media executions), onsite search, recipe networks, and retailer media networks (even though the retailer does offer onsite placements, they are limited).

The roof has been built. Now on to the pillars!

RANKING THE SIX PILLARS

. . .

Great news! You have some data on **PAST PERFORMANCE**. This makes your job so much easier and can guide your decision making for this program. It's your first pillar. However, it's not as straightforward as it seems.

You have two programs. One is almost identical to this execution, utilizing rich media ads that performed well. An in-stream audio was executed that was slightly different, based on timing (fall tailgating versus summer grilling) but generated a GMROI that was 52% stronger. To complicate matters, your budget is now below the threshold to get any statistically significant testing.

There isn't a wrong answer here; it's simple risk versus reward. The in-stream audio produced a much better GMROI, but was that unique to the season or to your tailgating message? Maybe. The summer program from last year met your success benchmark but didn't set the world on fire. However, there's no reason to think it wouldn't perform similarly again, so no risk of it being a major disappointment. On a $28,000 budget, your choice is to go with the higher reward option despite the risk. You choose **in-stream audio**. You also go with the same partner because you don't want to throw in any additional variables that could alter performance.

And you're done!

To recap this example:

. . .

KPI/Message:

Tactics: Ruled out digital display (less rich media), recipe networks, onsite search, and retailer media networks.

Partners: Ruled out digital display (less rich media), recipe networks, onsite search, and retailer media network partners.

1. PAST PERFORMANCE

Tactics: Ruled out video and rich media. **(IN- STREAM AUDIO IS YOUR CHOICE.)**

Partners: Ruled out video and rich media partners. **(YOUR PREVIOUS YEAR'S PARTNER IS YOUR CHOICE.)**

2. DATA: Did not factor in.

3. TECHNOLOGY: Did not factor in.

4. MEDIA: Did not factor in.

5. ATTRIBUTION: Did not factor in.

6. PRICING: Did not factor in.

BIBLIOGRAPHY

Introduction

Flint, Daniel J., et al. Shopper Marketing: Profiting from the Place Where Suppliers, Brand Manufacturers, and Retailers Connect. Pearson Education, 2014.

"Shopper Marketing: Step Up and Add Value." Engage Consultants, March 5, 2017, www.engageconsultants.com/recent/shopper-marketing-time-to-step-up/.

Stevens, Stanley, and Mars Digital. "Deloitte/GMA - Delivering the Promise of Shopper Marketing." Issuu, 2008, issuu.com/marsdigital/docs/gma-deloitte_shop permktreport_/16.

Data

Applift. "Deterministic vs. Probabilistic Data Tracking: Which Is More Effective?" *Applift*, June 18, 2019, applift. com/blog/deterministic-data.

TubeMogul. "Deterministic vs. Probabilistic Data". TubeMogul, September 8, 2016, https://www.tubemogul.com/wp-content/uploads/2016/09/Deterministic-vs-Probabilistic-Data.pdf.

Technology

Kilcourse, Brian. "Do Consumers Want Personalization or, Simply, Relevance?" Salesforce, blog, May 7, 2018, www.salesforce.com/blog/2018/05/consumers-want-personalization-simply-relevance.html.

Troy, Mike. "COVID-19 Accelerates Click and Collect Adoption." *Retail Leader*, Ensemble IQ, March 30, 2020, retailleader.com/covid-19-accelerates-click-and-collect-adoption.

Jay, Stefanie. "Walmart Media Group Summit." May 2018, San Francisco, California.

Media

Chicory. "Media and Advertising: Chicory." Chicory, 2020, chicory.co/advertisers.

Allrecipes. "Ad Services." *Allrecipes.com*, (Meredith Corporation) 2020, ads.allrecipes.com/ad-services/.

Attribution

Nielsen. "Beyond Clicks and Impressions: Examining the Relationship between Online Advertising and Brand Building," white paper, April 2019, https://www.nielsen.com/wp-content/uploads/sites/3/2019/04/Nielsen-Beyond-Clicks-and-Impressions.pdf.

Digital Media Tools in a Shopper Marketing World

Jackson Follow, Elizabeth. "Q4 Product Advertising Strategy for Retail Brand Manufacturers and Suppliers" LinkedIn SlideShare presentation, August 28, 2015, www.slideshare.net/CPCStrategy-ConvertRetailIntent/q4-product-advertising-strategy-for-retail-brand-manufacturers-suppliers.

Dade, F. M. *Blinded Independent Study on Digital Media Effectiveness in CPG*. 2020.

ABOUT THE AUTHOR

F. M. DADE has nearly two decades of marketing experience, primarily in the consumer packaged goods and shopper marketing spaces. He has worked on both sides of the house, as a seller of marketing solutions and client-side marketer. After a decade focusing on traditional media such as print and in-store signage, F. M. made the leap to the ad tech space, focusing on crafting platforms and product strategy around shopper marketing. From programmatic to social influencers to onsite search, he has sold or bought it all. He has worked for some of the most progressive ad tech firms and for (or with) some of the biggest brands in CPG. His digital media expertise has extended beyond CPG as he has spent time consulting or working for top firms in retail, auto, publishing, entertainment, travel and tourism, and nonprofit. But his heart will always be tied to shopper marketing. F. M. considers himself equally a Texan, a Chicagoan, and an Angeleno.

f